'In this compelling book, Cl[...] case for the claim that LGBT[...] Christian understandings [...] theological engagement with actual human stories. She gathers out of the fragments and promises of human lives fresh conceptions of hallowed relationships. A book for everyone – queer and straight – who longs to escape humbug and artificial holiness, and who wants to know more about how God blesses our lives and longings.'
                              – *Canon Rachel Mann, priest, poet and theologian*

'If the Church is to navigate the waters ahead, it will need the example of those like Clare who have shown what it means to listen, articulate, embody and let people make brave and unexpected journeys.'
                    – *Samuel Wells, Vicar of St Martin-in-the-Fields and Visiting Professor of Christian Ethics at King's College, London*

'It is a strange truth that it is when the Church is talking about loving relationships that it tries to be most controlling. Those who do not fit its acceptable categories quickly learn shame, anger, fear and, whilst wanting to be faithful Christians, know they are being seen as protesting radicals – which is the last thing they can feel inside. Who can open the window and let some fresh air in to this unhealthy and often hypocritical state of affairs? Well, Clare Herbert does in this excellent new book. With a heart that has come close to cracking, but which has been resuscitated by her partnership, she draws on the experience of those who want to love God and love their loved one with truth, integrity and hope. The result is an inspiriting, theologically informed and pastorally sensitive contribution to a conversation that needs all the help it can get. She shows in this project that by being heard, you hear yourself and, with love on your side, can hear the voice of God calling you into the better place.'
                    – *Mark Oakley, Dean of St John's College, Cambridge*

Towards a Theology of
Same-Sex Marriage

TOWARDS A THEOLOGY OF SAME-SEX MARRIAGE

SQUARING the CIRCLE

Clare Herbert

Foreword by Samuel Wells

Jessica Kingsley Publishers
London and Philadelphia

First published in Great Britain in 2021 by Jessica Kingsley Publishers
An Hachette Company

1

Copyright © Clare Herbert 2021
Foreword copyright © Samuel Wells 2021

The poem on page 45 '7301' by U.A. Fanthorpe is reproduced
with kind permission from Dr R.V. Bailey.
The poem on page 70 'Being Boring' by Wendy Cope is reproduced
with kind permission from Faber and Faber Ltd.
The poem on page 93 'Untitled Poem' by Thomas Merton, from *In The
Dark Before Dawn*, copyright © 1949 by Our Lady of Gethsemani Abbey
is reprinted by permission of New Directions Publishing Corp.

A CIP catalogue record for this title is available from the
British Library and the Library of Congress.

ISBN 978 1 78592 570 2
eISBN 978 1 78592 603 7

Printed and bound in Great Britain by Clays Ltd

Jessica Kingsley Publishers' policy is to use papers that are natural,
renewable and recyclable products and made from wood grown in
sustainable forests. The logging and manufacturing processes are expected
to conform to the environmental regulations of the country of origin.

Jessica Kingsley Publishers
Carmelite House
50 Victoria Embankment
London EC4Y 0DZ

www.jkp.com

Contents

Foreword

Clare Herbert is not a troublemaker. But she is a troublefinder. In the pages of this book we find a person of disarming humility, who listens profoundly, steps aside to let others' voices be heard, and summarizes her gleanings with assertive tenderness.

Clare once found herself excluded by a Church that had no ears to hear her call to ordination. She then found herself obscured and sometimes demonised by a Church that had no imagination to comprehend her sexuality. Yet she has retained a gentleness of spirit, glad for the gifts God has given her, and eager to receive and discern the gifts God is giving others. As Irenaeus put it, 'Keep your heart in a soft and malleable state so that you can feel the imprint of God's touch upon your life.' This book is a study in such receptivity.

For those who read this book in a mood of anger, hurt and pain, I say, you will find here a model of sober, generous, kind, patient engagement and understanding. There is anger here, most of it expressed in the words of those interviewed; but it is set alongside other reactions and emotions, within which context it has its worthy place. For those who read this book unsure of what the rapidly emerging vocabulary of gender and sexuality means and requires, I say, you will find here a healthy balance between the facility that handles complex concepts and the simplicity that understands the power of human testimony. Clare puts in conversation with one another the experience of those in same-sex civil partnerships, the wider Church discourse, her own witness, and the ever-strange, eternally wondrous workings of the Holy Spirit.

As you read, you will from time to time stop – moved deeply by a person's trust, or humanity, pain or insight. The book is a library of Christian feeling, fury, faith and fellowship. This is a testament from people who, without much support from family or society, and with scarcely any from the Church, have nonetheless found in union with one another a truth that must be told, recognised, heard and learned from; more than anything, admired. This is a book of love – durable, thrilling, surprising, sustained, genuine, powerful and transformative.

You will finish this book a wiser, kinder, more compassionate, more insightful person, somewhat in awe of the people whose stories it tells, and resolved to see some things in life and faith as simpler than they previously appeared; others more complex. If the Church is to navigate the waters ahead, it will need the example of those like Clare who have shown what it means to listen, articulate, embody, and let people make brave and unexpected journeys.

Is this not how the Holy Spirit works – to walk alongside, to surprise, to bring into new company, to disarm, to delight, to encourage, to transform? I pray that in reading this book you will have such an encounter with the Holy Spirit, the Spirit as Isaiah tells us, of wisdom and understanding, counsel and inward strength, knowledge and godly fear. Walk humbly: you are walking on holy ground.

Revd Dr Samuel Wells,
Vicar of St Martin-in-the-Fields

Acknowledgments

My life has been enriched and supported by many people. So, there is a sense in which they are all part of this book. But there are some to whom I owe a huge debt of gratitude.

I am grateful for the friendship and encouragement of the clergy and congregation of St Martin-in-the-Fields. Among them I am indebted to two Vicars of St Martin's, the Right Reverend Nicholas Holtam and the Reverend Dr Sam Wells, and to the participants in my doctoral research. Without their enthusiastic support I would not have had the courage to make this journey.

My tutors in the Cambridge Theological Federation Colleges and Anglia Ruskin University inspired and helped me to achieve the doctorate in practical theology which undergirds the writing of this book. More importantly, they convinced me that I have an authoritative theological voice of my own which merits hearing. They are Zoe Bennet, Philomena Cullen, Vernon Trafford, Sebastian Rasinger and David Lyall.

My friends and family have walked with me through years of research and writing, wondering how I could possibly take so long to complete one doctorate and write one book. Particular thanks are due to Louise Hide, Gillian Clarke and Tati Howell who corrected the text; to David Flagg, my colleague at St Augustine's College of Theology, who encouraged me to publish; and to Alan Gregory, Principal of St Augustine's who generously gave me space one summer to complete my writing.

Finally, this book is dedicated to Philippa Garety, without whose love it is impossible for me to imagine living, without whose enquiring faith my life would be impoverished, and without whose confidence in me little written about here would have been accomplished.

For the last six years I have worked as a tutor in pastoral theology. Nothing convinces me more of the importance of this book, and others like it, than the lives and strivings of gifted ordinands, who long to love God, their vocation, and their same-sex partner. I am grateful to them for their trust in me, and their hope for a future lived more openly, joyfully and faithfully, as this book envisages, and as I hope for them.

Introduction

Once, in a secure glass case at an art exhibition, I glimpsed a rare object: a circle which had been squared. It was a marriage cup made of gold, of rose-gold and of silver, with square base and round rim, designed by the Russian jeweller Fabergé. The square base supported a cup sufficiently stable to resist being toppled in haste. Yet the round rim invited the lips of lovers to seal their commitment to each other with a shared sip of wine. The vessel was beautiful to view from all angles, as the light changed, glancing off the different constituent metals, which gleamed and shone as the visitor walked around it. It was, like a good marriage, an invitation to the joy of contemplating something rare and beautiful, richly textured, burnished by the touch of years.

When I was growing into adulthood, and realizing my sexual orientation to be lesbian, it was impossible for me to imagine being contentedly married. Furthermore, to reconcile same-sex relationships with the Christian concept of marriage was simply inconceivable. It was like trying to think of a square circle, and to long, painfully, to possess that to which nothing corresponded in my mind's eye.

Yet the idea of a squared circle has symbolic reality. For the idea encourages us to imagine that which we think unimaginable. This book's subtitle *Squaring the Circle* is an attempt to describe the seeming impossibility of naming together in one breath God and gay, Christian marriage and same-sex partnership. This book invites us to take a journey together, through territory sometimes familiar and safe, sometimes unknown and strange, a journey into imagining the unimaginable.

The purpose of the journey

The journey begins with trouble: trouble at the threshold of the Church, where we step over from Church to world and back again, and where the realms of Church and the surrounding society merge or clash, join and divide. The shape of the trouble is a storm blowing through the Church of England and other, though not all, Christian churches, over the quality and status of long-term committed same-sex relationships.[1] The storm rumbles over my own head.

On New Year's Eve, as bell-ringers prepared to ring out the old year and ring in the new, and as fireworks began to explode all around, I conducted a wedding. The celebration held great significance for the bride and groom, since they had waited to find that person with whom each felt 'at home'. More poignantly, the bride had suffered such serious illness in recent years that her family and friends had once feared for her life. For all of us gathered, this was an occasion of hope, of huge joy and thankfulness, and for me a privilege to be asked to conduct the ceremony.

I knew the bride because my partner of thirty years is a lifelong friend of the family. Yet, ironically and painfully, I am unable to marry my own partner, since I am a priest in the Church of England. As a priest, I am permitted by canon law to belong with my partner in a civil partnership, yet not to be married. While I enjoy conducting weddings, I may neither bless the civil marriage of same-sex couples, nor marry those same couples in church. The reason for these prohibitions, explored further in Chapter 1 and Chapter 6 of this book, is that the Church of England remains firmly committed to the traditional doctrine of marriage: that marriage can only take

---

1   The position of the Church of England regarding same-sex marriage, and its relationship with other Christian churches and societies in England and Wales, is fully explained in Chapter 1. Here it is important to note that there exist churches within the Anglican Communion where same-sex marriage is celebrated, notably the Episcopal Church in the United States of America and, nearer to hand, the Scottish Episcopal Church.

place between a man and a woman, and that such marriage is the
sole context in which sexual intercourse should take place. These
beliefs cause enormous tensions for gay and lesbian people, whether
they wish to be married in church like their heterosexual friends,
or simply wish the Church to be a place where equality for gay and
lesbian people is recognized. I explore the impact on gay and lesbian
people of these beliefs in this book, as well as the positive routes
taken by gay and lesbian Christians to love both God and their life-
partners. I ask the question whether it is possible and desirable for
the Church of England, and other churches in similar positions, to
move towards an understanding of long-term committed same-sex
relationships as marriage.

This is a book of human stories like my own, which reflect the lives
of Christians bearing in their bodies, minds and spirits the struggle
to love both God and their life-partner, who yet refuse to relinquish
either love. In *A Conversation Waiting to Begin* Oliver O'Donovan asks
the question 'What good news does the gay Christian have to bring the
Church?' (2009, p.103). Here he echoes another question put by Rowan
Williams, 'How does the homosexually inclined person show Christ to
the world?' (2003, p.18). This book asks such questions about the living
witness to faith of gay and lesbian Christians. Reflecting on my story, a
Christian priest of the Church of England who is lesbian, and who has
flourished for thirty years in a relationship of loving commitment and
faithfulness, and on the stories of 13 gay and lesbian Christians who
worked with me as research participants in writing this book, I suggest
that our stories attest to a living faith, and our relationships illuminate
meanings of Christian marriage.

Perhaps a word of reassurance is necessary. You will not find here
a set of stories from people who regard themselves as victims, and
who consequently demand marriage purely as a matter of healing
and, even legitimately, of justice. The majority of those whose stories
you will read are happily fulfilled in their relationships, and yet do
not cast off the Church as outrageously conservative. Nor do they
reject the claims of a transcendent kingdom of God. Instead, they
strive to place their flourishing relationships in the light of their
understanding of God. They search both Church tradition and
the Bible to comprehend where holiness may lie, using their own

experience as a rich gift with which to test the moral truth of both. This book is therefore an interweaving of experience, my own experience and that of other participants in the book, with broader theological and secular concerns. For those with academic interests, the book is *hermeneutic* in content, concerned with the interpretation of marriage, and the meaning of same-sex relationships.

At the journey's end my hope is that you will be able to join a conversation about the theological meanings of same-sex marriage with fresh understanding. The challenge of where the journey ends – whether you are LGBTQ[2] or straight, whether you are of Christian, or another faith, or none, whether you are an experienced church minister or a new student of theology – lies in continuing to talk to each other across differences of opinion and belief.

A map for the journey

In Chapter 1 of this book, 'Faith on a Landslide', I describe how my own life story led me to ask the question at the heart of this book, which is how to reconcile an understanding of the love of God with the love experienced by same-sex partners in their relationships of long-term commitment and intimacy. I explain here the context of my question, which is the tension experienced by gay and lesbian Christians, their families and friends, between the increased tolerance of homosexuality in British society, culminating in the Marriage (Same Sex Couples) Act of 2013, and the disapproval of same-sex marriage voiced in the formal statements of many churches including the Catholic Church and the Church of England. I explain how I decided to resolve this tension for myself by conducting a piece of research in practical theology at the church of St Martin-in-the-Fields in Trafalgar Square, where I worked for five years as Assistant Priest and Lecturer in Inclusive Theology.

---

2   Since the 1980s the word *gay* in the term *gay community* has been replaced by the initials LGB, LGBT and LGBTQ. The initials LGBTQ stand for Lesbian, Gay, Bisexual, Transgender and Queer/Questioning. While aware of the recent expansion of this initialism to LGBTQIA+ I continue to use the initials LGBTQ in this book since they cover the spectrum of research participants' initials of self-identification at the time of interview.

On a map we discover straightforward roads and paths. We may also encounter surprises, even obstacles to surmount when we plan a route. You will encounter the first surprise in this book in the very first chapter. For in that chapter you will find that my research process began in 2010. At that time, in the narrow period of history between 2005 and 2014, civil partnership constituted the only status recognized in the civil law of England and Wales available to gay and lesbian couples wishing to make a permanent commitment to each other. My research was therefore conducted among gay and lesbian congregation members worshipping regularly at St Martin-in-the-Fields who were not yet married, but in relationships of civil partnership. I interviewed a group of seven women aged between 25 and 55, whose names are disguised for the sake of anonymity, but who in this book are called Anne, Christina, Emma, Lillian, Lucy, Sue and Vanessa. Five of the group self-identified in their interview as lesbian, one as bisexual, and one as gender queer. All seven self-identified as White British. At the time of their interview they worked in professions that included Higher Education, Public Service, Administration, and the Arts. I worked in the same way with a group of six men, aged between 30 and 60, who are called in this book David, Matthew, Robert, Stephen, Ted and Tom. Three of the group self-identified as White British, two as White Other and one as White Asian. Four of the men were interviewed face to face, and two responded in writing instead to questionnaires containing the interview questions. All six men, who worked at the time of interview in the fields of Law, Higher Education, Management Consultancy, and Business, self-identified as gay or homosexual. All 13 participants enjoyed relationships of civil partnership that had been celebrated, by some quietly, by others noisily, by some at a register office, by others also in services of prayer and dedication in church.

How relevant is it, in a book concerning the theology of same-sex marriage, to describe research into the meaning of civil partnership? This is a relevant area of research for two reasons. First, because the registration of civil partnership was a new rite, untried in secular society, and attended by no authorized liturgy of the Church, its meaning was there to be created in the minds of my research participants. Did they see it as marriage? Second, because it had not yet met with warm approval in the official statements of the Church of England, which is the context of this research, I was able to explore theological meanings that give motivation to a minority creating its own theology alongside the formally stated theology of the Church. I was able to identify a new theology of marriage as it was being made. Therefore, in Chapter 2, 'Outward and Visible Sign', I investigate the sacramental nature of long-term same-sex relationships of commitment and intimacy and suggest that signs of the presence of God are visible here. Similarly, in Chapter 3, 'Escape from Wilderness', I find the research participants bearing witness to the liberating activity of God experienced in and through their relationships.

Another possible challenge awaits you in Chapter 4, 'Something Borrowed, Something New'. For there you will discover that I interrogated the conversations with my research participants for signs of queer theology. This may surprise you, even shock you, since the word *queer* scares or attracts readers in equal measure, for its resonance with strangeness and aberration. Queer theology, which is explored in Chapter 4, is a stepping-stone on the journey where you may feel initially unsafe, or alternatively excited and intrigued. For queer theology borrows language and methodology from queer theory, which is concerned to explore the ways in which heterosexuality is privileged as normal, or even as ideal, in our society. When used of God, the word *queer* describes both the 'outsider' places and people that act as contexts for the revelation of God in Judeo-Christian religious tradition, and the sense of God as ineffable, beyond definition, a challenge to all human attempts to manipulate the power and meaning of God for the benefit of self. I used queer theology as a tool to enable me to seek hidden voices and thoughts not always heard in mainstream theological debate. The research required an instrument sufficiently broad and sharp to knock my own social and theological preconceptions off balance, and to help me see the meanings of relationships and the meanings of God through new eyes. Only if I found such an instrument would I be able to establish what is theologically unique here.

In Chapter 5, 'Enduring Love', I discover fragments of a theology of same-sex marriage before considering in Chapter 6, 'Pause for

Thought', conflicting views and opposing arguments to my own. In this chapter I suggest how both the Bible and Christian tradition are read with seriousness by the research participants, while they honour the role of human experience in ethical decision making and the creation of theology.

Finally, in Chapter 7, 'A Space for the Heart', I conclude that it is possible to detect among the fragments assembled in this book a confident, joyful queer theology of marriage to share, debate, overthrow, or enjoy. I invite you to enter the journey with me, to explore the possibility that Christian same-sex marriage may not fall short of the ideal, or simply be justified, but may also offer new understandings of God and human love. In short, the circle may be squared.

Chapter 1

FAITH ON A LANDSLIDE

A personal story

A step leads to the front door of Centrepoint, which I knew as a hostel for homeless people, at 54 Dean Street, Soho. One evening a man sat waiting on that step, shielding his face with a baseball cap. When he heard an explosion, he hurried away into the surrounding network of streets. That man was David Copeland. The explosion he caused on 30 April 1999, with a nail bomb held together with human excrement, ripped apart the Admiral Duncan pub, a gay bar on Old Compton Street. He killed three adults and an unborn child, injuring 70 others. Victims of the bomb lost limbs. Others began a life of slow-burning infection caused by the excrement hidden within the bomb. The bomb was created by a person willing to murder and maim others whom he considered to be outsiders and inferior to the white British heterosexual norm. He had recently targeted London's Asian and African Caribbean populations. Now it was the turn of the gay community and their friends.

At the time of the explosion I was the Rector of St Anne's Church, at 55 Dean Street, Soho. The step where David Copeland sat was next to the entrance of the church and of my home. His action affected me deeply, as it did the church and the community we served. The community was shocked, injured and bereaved. The parish church threw open its gates, never to close them again against the discussion of the issues surrounding homosexuality and the Christian faith. I had been deeply troubled by the question of how to reconcile my lesbian identity with the vocation of priest within the Church of

England. Panic attacks had attended my struggle to comprehend how my relationship of love with my partner was essentially different from the love known by heterosexual people within marriage. Now I discovered for the first time how my identity as Church of England priest and lesbian might help me understand the pastoral care needed by families bereaved by the bombing. For such families not only faced the acute pain of sudden loss, but also became embroiled overnight in bewilderment, and in some cases shame, over how to explain to others why their dear ones might spend time drinking in a gay bar. I began to understand how my life experience proves a vantage point in ministry among the community committed to my care. Such glimmers of personal integrity were rare.

I was born in 1954. My formative years were spent in an isolated rural community of conservative Christian views. Sex outside marriage was completely taboo. Women achieved adult status by being married and bearing children, and for the most part remaining at home in farm or cottage. To be single, not to be affirmed by men as sufficiently desirable for marriage, was to have missed the point of being female, and to be the butt of sometimes gentle, sometimes cruel humour. I gained a boyfriend quickly in my teenage years to avert these horrors, but I fell behind in self-esteem as I grew away from my local peers at school and university. Church became a haven for me, a place where my creativity and leadership skills flourished, where pressure decreased to perform well sexually, since the zealous commitment to the life of Church of a young single woman met approval.

Through university and early employment, contradictory experiences rendered me always slightly depressed until I discovered feminism in my late twenties. I was confused that my own main affective relationships were with women rather than with men. I received offers of marriage while realizing that I had no distinct and happy sense of myself flourishing within those relationships. Throughout these years, the Church of England remained a fruitful place of belonging for me, where I wanted to live my professional life. Yet that choice too created conflict for me, since I enjoyed and excelled in training for ministry, yet was unable as a woman to be ordained priest. In the 1980s, in circles of women exploring feminist theology, I discovered both my place to stand in theological integrity and my own lesbian identity. As

I grew older and more experienced in ministry, by carefully choosing certain Church posts, and by sharing my inner fears with a skilled psychotherapist, I was able to survive, if not enjoy, being both lesbian and an ordained minister within the Church of England.

In my own life, the event that at once 'outed' me as lesbian, whilst affirming among family and friends the choices I had made about a long-term committed relationship, was my own entry into civil partnership in 2006. I had had time to reflect on the value of this relationship, its liberating and grounding effect on my faith, my partner's support of my vocation, and our joint responsibilities to care not only for each other but for a multitude of family and friends, since we had been living together for 15 years. As I reflected on that rite it seemed quite unexpectedly, both on the day itself and in its future implications, very like marriage. I felt sure that I knew the presence of God in both my priestly vocation and in my relationship with my partner, and that one indeed supported the capacity to fulfil the other. Yet I knew too the struggle to live with and challenge official Church views, since civil I had agreed with diocesan officials not to openly publish news of our celebration of civil partnership in the parish of which I was incumbent. As I reflected over how theology influenced my decision to enter and continue this partnership, and how the partnership influenced the development of my own faith and vocation, I glimpsed a question I needed to answer, which is the question at the heart of this book: how may we reconcile an understanding of the love of God and the love experienced by same-sex partners in relationships of long-term commitment? Is it possible to square the circle? May we conceive a confident, joyous theology of same-sex marriage, and understand how this contributes to a richer understanding of marriage and to our knowledge of the God seen in the face of Jesus? The question does not belong to me alone. It fascinates, irritates, stimulates and repels Christians and non-Christians alike, as we explore its far-reaching implications.

A shared question: The role of the state

In his novel *The Emperor Waltz* (2014), Philip Hensher explores the theme of passionate love in such disparate contexts as a third-century Roman outpost, the city of Berlin in the 1930s, and a hospital in contemporary London. Marriage is described from the diverse perspectives of characters living in these varying contexts. A Christian martyr finds her pagan marriage oppressive, preferring to live in prison among believers, and to die for love of Christ, than to remain a pampered, voiceless possession of her despotic husband. A craftsman father and his home-maker daughter marry their spouses for the sake of wealth, rather than for love, when inflation gallops, threatening starvation in its wake, in Germany between the two world wars. In contemporary London, a hospital patient casually mentions that the frequent male visitor to his bedside is his husband. The novel was published in 2014. It shows how there have been dynamic shifts in the nature and meaning of marriage in the West.

In September 2011, following the 2010 General Election, the Liberal Democrat Minister for Equalities announced that the Coalition government of the United Kingdom would launch a consultation in March 2012 on how to introduce civil marriage for same-sex couples in England and Wales. The consultation closed in June 2012 and, in December 2012, the new Minister for Women and Equalities announced that the government would be introducing legislation within the lifetime of the parliamentary session. The Marriage (Same Sex Couples) Bill was introduced into Parliament on 24 January 2013. The Bill received its Second Reading on 5 February 2013, passing by a large majority of 400 to 175, and its Third Reading in the House of Commons on 21 May 2013, passing with a majority of 366 to 161.

In the House of Lords, the Bill received its First Reading on 21 May 2013 and passed its Second Reading on 3 and 4 June 2013, after a vote of 390 votes to 148. The Bill was supported, and a wrecking amendment rejected, by a majority from every party with representation in the House. The final vote of almost 3–1 against the amendment, and in favour of the Bill as it stood, was described by media and other observers as 'very remarkable'. The Queen granted Royal Assent to the Bill on 17 July 2013, which thereby became the Marriage (Same Sex Couples) Act 2013.

The overwhelming support for this Bill reflected the speed and force with which attitudes towards homosexuality had changed since 1967, when private homosexual acts between men over the age of

21 were decriminalized in England and Wales. Milestones along the way were these:

- In 1992, when the World Health Organization declassified same-sex attraction as a mental illness.
- In 1994, when the age of consent for men was lowered to 18 (and in 2000 to 16).
- In 2002, when new adoption legislation gave unmarried and same-sex couples the right to adopt, while the Civil Partnerships Bill 2002 was introduced as a private members' bill in the House of Lords, and passed its Second Reading.
- In 2003, when the Employment Equality (Sexual Orientation) Regulations rendered it illegal to discriminate against gay, lesbian or bisexual people in the workplace.
- Again in 2003, when *Civil Partnership: A Framework for the Legal Recognition of Same-sex Couples* was published as a consultation document by the Women and Equality Unit of the Department of Trade and Industry. In this document, government proposals for the registration of civil partnership were set out for the first time.
- In 2004, when responses to that consultation paper revealed that 84 per cent welcomed the idea of a civil partnership registration scheme so that in November 2004, Royal Assent was given to the Civil Partnership Act 2004.
- In 2007, when the Equality Act (Sexual Orientation) Regulations outlawed discrimination in the provision of goods, services and education.

Of these, the Civil Partnership Act 2004 was perhaps the most significant, for now civil partnerships were granted rights and responsibilities identical to those of civil marriage. Civil partners therefore became entitled to the same rights as married couples with regard to property ownership and tenancy, inheritance tax, social security and pension benefits, parental responsibility for a partner's children, maintenance of partner and children, life insurance recognition and next-of-kin rights. The dissolution of partnerships was also given formal legal process. It seemed as if a massive turning point had arrived in the history of gay rights with civil partnership legislation and its public celebration. The media exploded with stories and photographs of beaming same-sex couples, their families and friends, enjoying the first legally sanctioned and publicly approved rites of passage for gay and lesbian people. Ten years later, in 2015 – by which time almost 140,000 people had entered into civil partnership in the UK – Ben Summerskill, the former chief executive of Stonewall, suggested to the BBC that it had 'paved the way as a test run for many of the gay rights granted in the following decade' (Hutton 2015).

The use of the title 'Faith on a Landslide' for this chapter describes my dizzying experience of living with these personally liberating changes that reveal a vastly increased tolerance to homosexuality in civil society, while I searched for solid footholds in faith. In 1957, when I was three years old, the Wolfenden Committee had recommended the decriminalization of homosexual acts performed privately between two men who had reached the age of 21. Ten years later, when I was entering puberty and wondering doubtingly if I would ever be married, the Sexual Offences Act changed life overnight both legally and socially for those living secretly in homosexual partnerships. In 2006, after a lifetime of coming to terms with not being married, finding myself instead in a long-term committed lesbian partnership, I entered a civil partnership. On 17 July 2013, the Marriage (Same Sex Couples) Bill received Royal Assent, so that by now, at 60, I could choose to be married. What had led to these changes in law?

In his work *The Transformation of Intimacy* the sociologist Anthony Giddens suggests that five developments in social, scientific and political thought have been catalysts creating change in attitudes to sexuality in the West. Since the industrial revolution the sheer increase in material well-being and access to goods led to a greater emphasis on the importance of individual choice in decisions about lifestyle. Then, in the 19th and 20th centuries there was a decline in religious belief and in the value of former social constraints, especially where these were not understood to lead to a sense of personal fulfilment. Significantly, the human sciences led to the development of contraceptive medicine so that sexual activity was released from its connection with the procreation of children in the minds of many people. The same sciences contributed to an increasingly popular view that there is a natural diversity of sexual preference within the human population, and that for some people erotic attraction and sexual orientation are neither chosen nor easily changed. Then, the concept of sexual orientation emerged over the last two centuries, so that the understanding of homosexuality as a matter of personal identity, whether essential or constructed, lifelong or transitory, gradually gained popular acceptance in Western countries. At the same time, our understanding of marriage has undergone subtle changes, so that there is now a widespread decrease in emphasis on distinct gender roles, or the social conventions connected to wealth and property transmission, and more value placed on its companionate nature, and its capacity for emotional intimacy (Giddens 1992, pp.26–28).

These evolutions in social thought and behaviour were among those that led to the perception of restrictions on gay and lesbian activity being considered unnecessary and oppressive. Ultimately, they led to the landslide votes of approval for the Marriage (Same Sex Couples) Bill in both the House of Commons and the House of Lords. Civil marriage for same-sex partners became a choice for couples in England and Wales in 2013. It is now, in 2019, recognized by law in 29 countries of the world.

A shared question: The role of the Church

As early as 2009, Quakers in Britain, the Society of Friends, decided to campaign for the right to marry same-sex couples in Quaker meetings for worship, having considered the issues surrounding same-sex relationships for many years. In 2016, the United Reformed Church became the largest Christian denomination in the UK to freely permit the celebration and registration of same-sex couples in its churches. In 2019, the Methodist Church, the UK's fourth largest Christian denomination, consented in principle to the marriage of same-sex couples while they await a final vote on the issue in July 2020. The two largest denominations, however, the Church of England and the Roman Catholic Church, stood firmly against the legalization of same-sex marriage.

The House of Bishops of the Church of England reacted to the Civil Partnership Act with a majority voting for its rejection in the House of

Lords, and then, when it was passed, with pastoral caution. This careful reaction, impeding neither lay nor clergy members of the Church of England from entering civil partnerships, was predicated upon the understanding that such partnerships between Christians should be celibate in nature if involving clergy, and was not even between lay people to be considered the ideal setting for sexual intercourse, since this, 'as an expression of faithful intimacy, properly belongs within marriage exclusively' (Church of England 2005). Nevertheless, with the advent of the Civil Partnership Act, handfuls of informally created services of prayer, dedication, thanksgiving, and, in some cases, full services of blessing that resembled marriage liturgies, for same-sex couples were welcomed for use in some churches. These services of prayer and dedication were offered in response to the lines in the 2005 Bishops' Statement that requests for prayer should be approached with pastoral sensitivity to suit the needs of individual couples.

This cautious quiet was blown away by the Coalition government's publication on 15 March 2012 of an Equalities Office consultation on lifting the ban against same-sex civil marriage. This precipitated an atmosphere of crisis in the Church of England, which culminated in a very long and forthright statement in response to the consultation, made on 12 June 2012, in which the Church of England stated that it 'cannot support the proposal to enable "all couples, regardless of their gender, to have a civil marriage ceremony"', and pointed out that 'such a change would alter the intrinsic nature of marriage as the union of a man and a woman, as enshrined in human institutions throughout history' (Church of England 2012).

When the Bill entered its Second Reading in the House of Lords, of the 14 bishops able to vote, nine voted against the Bill and five abstained from voting. So strong were voices of religious opposition that when the Marriage (Same Sex Couples) Bill was passed in Parliament a 'quadruple lock' was inserted into the Bill to safeguard religious organizations from being forced to conduct same-sex marriages. The quadruple lock would:

- ensure that no religious organization or individual minister can be compelled to marry same-sex couples or to permit this to happen on their premises

- provide an opt-in system for religious organizations who wish to conduct marriages for same-sex couples
- amend the Equality Act 2010 to reflect that no discrimination claims can be brought against religious organizations or individual ministers for refusing to marry a same-sex couple
- ensure that legislation will not affect the canon law of the Church of England or the Church in Wales.

As a result of the final element of the quadruple lock, if either church wanted to conduct a same-sex marriage, it would require a change to primary legislation at a later date, and a change to canon law. Religious groups that wished to opt in to holding same-sex ceremonies included at that time the Unitarians and the Society of Friends, but individual leaders in such congregations and meetings would be free to opt out. Equally, if an Anglican vicar wished to hold a same-sex marriage at a time when the Church was opposed to such marriage, that ceremony would not be recognized in law.

The official view of the Roman Catholic Church towards same-sex unions is similarly unambiguous. The English text of the report of the Synod on the Family, which was published on 30 October 2014, contained the words 'There are absolutely no grounds for considering homosexual unions to be in any way similar to or even remotely analogous to God's plan for marriage and the family'. The words are a quotation from an earlier document, released by the Vatican on 31 July 2003, which condemned the legalization of same-sex marriages and called upon Catholic politicians to vote against it (Congregation for the Doctrine of the Faith 2003).

The theologies of marriage of the Church of England and of the Roman Catholic Church, which supports these prohibitions, and which are based in considerations of the authority of Scripture and Church tradition, is given serious and close attention in Chapter 6 of this book, which is entitled 'Pause for Thought: Conflicting Views and Opposing Arguments'. Their importance in this chapter, as theologies of the two largest Christian denominations in the UK, lies in their giving the context for LGBTQ Christians sensing that they live faith 'on a landslide', aware that their closest relationships may not earn the approval, let alone the blessing, of the churches to which they belong. Tension is increased for worshippers in the Church of England by the awareness that same-sex couples may look forward to the celebration of their marriage in other churches of the worldwide Anglican Communion, including the Episcopal Church in the USA since 2015 and, much closer to home, the Episcopal Church of Scotland since 2017.

Moving forward

Caught in the tension between strongly opposing worldviews and theological perspectives, I carried my question with me when I moved to minister as Assistant Priest and Lecturer in Inclusive Theology at St Martin-in-the-Fields in 2010. It was a fortunate move. The very architecture of St Martin's is designed to square circles, to permit different and clashing philosophies, theologies and political allegiances to flourish under one roof.

James Gibbs, an architect from Aberdeen who was a closet Catholic, yet who had been building Protestant churches in London, imagined the unimaginable when he designed St Martin-in-the-Fields between 1722 and 1726 to be a new royal parish church. He built it for George I, the new Hanoverian King, who had been invited to London to rule over the new United Kingdom of Great Britain, which was formed by the uniting of England with Scotland in 1707. Gibbs forged a new architectural language where the different traditions of the English church could co-exist. He married the classical style of a Roman portico, and the Scottish emphasis on the power of the Word preached from a high pulpit, with an English spire. He represented Catholicism, Protestantism and Anglicanism in the architecture of one commanding building. This new architectural shape, which ought, in its mixture of architectural styles, to offend the eye and conflict the senses, did the exact opposite. It reconciled warring factions for tolerating and sustaining life together in a new world.

The congregation of St Martin's is 'broad church' in theological outlook, so attracts members from all three branches of the Church of England: liberal, evangelical and catholic. It does so both because it is a popular place of welcome to visitors from across the world, and because it takes a radical stance on issues of social justice and emphasizes the importance of asking theological questions about statements of faith. Both visitors to London and Londoners moving out of their parish church to seek this radical questioning stance are attracted to belong. Shortly after I arrived, the welcome to the Lesbian Gay Bisexual and Trans community was expressly mentioned in its Mission Statement. As a result, that community was strongly represented in the membership, and we conducted services of prayer and thanksgiving following civil partnership for same-sex couples who were well known to the church.

In my new post, I resolved to share with the staff team and the congregation my question of how to reconcile my awareness of the love of God with the experience of love within a long-term committed same-sex relationship. I decided to conduct a piece of research in practical theology.

A foothold on the journey: Research in practical theology

Practical theology values contemporary experience as a source of theology. It uses human experience to converse with and interrogate traditional theologies while expecting those same theologies to probe and question human experience as 'a location of radiant immanence in which we may find God' (Bennett *et al.* 2018). It allowed me to investigate my own experience and that of others as theologically significant while recognizing Scripture and tradition as authoritative conversation partners in the search for God's revelation. Practical theology also recognizes that conversations about God interest people outside the Church as well as people within it. There are those outside the Church who may be both mystified by the apparent difficulty of accepting same-sex marriage, when the Church is so clearly interested in maintaining the importance of the institution of marriage in society, and keen to ask the question of whether same-sex marriage might not add new theological insights to more traditional understandings. However, practical theology itself contains many subdivisions of theme, content, method, research method and methodology. I was faced with the question of what branch of practical theology would take me on the next step on the journey.

In my work as a parish priest in Soho, I noticed that gay and lesbian people rarely sought my pastoral care understood as therapeutic. Certainly, I was never asked to heal their sexual identity or orientation. Rather, their life situations threw up for them urgent questions of meaning, which they wished to discuss with me in the context of Christian belief. When asking me to bless their relationship, the underlying question was, usually, 'Does God's grace extend to us and our concerns?' When asking me to take care of their family after their death, and at their funeral, the underlying question was, typically, 'Is the family of the Church sufficiently spacious to accommodate my family, who are warring over the meaning of my life?' When asking if they should seek ordination, the underlying question was always 'Do you think my own interpretation of my life's meaning will coincide with the meaning the Church of England may give to my life story?' They came seeking to discuss whether the stories of their lives coincided or clashed with the stories of God and the Church, as I understood those stories, as they perceived me to be a person who had already considered how the meaning of my life story coincided with the Christian story of God. The pastoral care I offered was hermeneutic, in the sense that it consisted of conversations concerning the meaning of events and experiences.

The question at the heart of this book is similar to the pastoral questions I encountered in my ministry. It is a question about meaning. It is a question related to the lived experience of lesbian and gay Christians in the context of their faith and relationships, which in turn are shaped by, and shape, church and society. It is a question about subjectivity, about how we are shaped and conditioned by the outer world, and about how we then shape that world. Moreover, there is a clear link with my own life story. Not only was I living the question, but in the research process that followed, participants perceived me as 'one who knows' about being part of the LGBTQ community, about being in a civil partnership, about theology, about the official statements and theology of the Church of England. I was not detached from the question to be explored but engaged in it from the perspective of my own life. The sociologist Tim May describes such engaged and committed researchers thus: 'We are no longer proclaiming our "disengagement" from our subject matter as a condition of science (positivism), but our "commitment" and "engagement" as a condition of understanding social life' (2001, p.15). May then describes how hermeneutics, which is the branch of knowledge that deals with interpretation, refers not only to the theory and practice of interpretation, but also to the ways in which our own understanding and interpretation of our own social world are 'necessary conditions for us to undertake research'. This description was congruent with one of the aims of this research, which was to challenge and deepen my own understanding of the theological meaning of the relationship at the heart of my life. I therefore decided to conduct a piece of research in hermeneutical practical theology.

To do this, I conducted a series of interviews with the 13 Christians worshipping regularly at St Martin-in-the-Fields described in the Introduction. I wanted to find for myself what theological meanings they gave to their relationships of civil partnership, to the civil registration ceremony itself, and to other surrounding rites that may have been celebrated in church. My aim was to discover whether I could identify in their stories a coherent theology, or fragments of theology. Did their relationships have connections with faith, and if so, what were these connections?

I interrogated the conversations for signs of a theology of marriage. I did this for four reasons. First, since the government's consultation on same-sex marriage was continuing even while this research was conducted, it was likely that my research participants would mention marriage. Second, the press ran with the similarities between civil partnership and marriage from the very beginning of their coverage of civil partnership ceremonies. Third, marriage registrars immediately underlined the similarity between civil partnership and civil marriage by distributing to potential civil partners administrative forms and 'orders of ceremony' precisely the same as those available for the celebration of civil marriage. Last, and perhaps most significantly, marriage remains the most meaningful institution to signify long-term commitments of love between adults, and I found that marriage was therefore alluded to frequently in the three practice interviews that I conducted in the context of another city and congregation, which I used to refine my interview content and skills.

Finally, not wishing to represent my own views in the questions that led to the conversations, and in the participants' answers, I carefully coded the conversations, breaking them down to individual units of meaning, and analysed them by theme. To conduct this research process I used a method of thematic analysis described by the psychologists Braun and Clarke (2013). I wanted to ensure that the theological beliefs of ordinary gay and lesbian people who are faithful members of a Christian congregation, yet whose voices are not always heard in the official statements of the churches, came to the foreground, while I accepted my own background role in the creation and maintenance of the process of interview.

I invite you now to follow the journey of what the congregation members said, and of my interpretation of their responses to my questions about the meaning of their relationships. In these research participants' voices I found evidence of a God who appears to choose to be known and addressed outside heteronormative patterns of love. The intriguing question remains: do we hear in these voices descriptions of marriage, or not?

Chapter 2

OUTWARD AND VISIBLE SIGN

In relation to our growth, it's not like I am not married, not involved in this prophetic work…

Matthew (research participant)

Transformative effects

On Saturday 18 February 2006 I entered into a civil partnership. I arrived early at the hairdresser, where I experienced the intense pleasure and nervous anxiety which coloured the whole day. Pleasure sprang from the hairdresser's kindness. He would give me my haircut as a 'wedding present'. My anxieties were aroused when I glimpsed, behind me in the mirror, the smiling face of a member of the congregation. Despite my careful plans to keep this event quiet in my parish, given the cautious attitude to civil partnership in the Church of England, the cat was now well and truly 'out of the bag'.

The registration of a civil partnership is a public event. Though it is true that the couple concerned simply need to sign a document for the registration to be complete, this signing nevertheless takes place before two registrars, who represent the civil law, and in the presence of two witnesses. Before the signing ceremony takes place, the law requires that notice of the registration be displayed publicly in the register office for a minimum period of 28 days so that the couple's freedom to enter a civil partnership may be openly contested or confirmed. If the couple wishes to hold a fuller celebration than this simple signing, they are invited by the registrars to choose between rites very close in structure and language to civil marriage ceremonies. To these they may add their own vows, readings, poems and music, which are forbidden in law to demonstrate religious content. The number of guests invited, and therefore the size of the public celebration, is a decision of the couple.

Among the research participants 11 enjoyed large, noisy public events to celebrate their civil partnership registration. Two participants chose to celebrate more quietly. Yet significantly this couple had carefully and deliberately informed their whole family and friendship circle of their new relationship status. In the stories about their civil partnerships, a common, striking feature is that the public nature of the rite is itself experienced as transformative of the person concerned and of their ensuing relationship. The transformative effects described are these: a strengthening of self-identity; a clarification of relationship status; an act of justice seeking; and the challenge to the religious and social taboo still surrounding homosexuality.

The strengthening of self-identity

How do gay and lesbian people publicly communicate their identity and declare the significance of their intimate relationships? When I first recognized my own sexual orientation in the early 1980s, safe places for lesbian self-expression were few. I recognized the anger of one interviewee, Anne. She was enraged by being considered simply 'single'. Anne states:

> I still get members of my family, you know, sending me Christmas cards addressed to me as Miss!

I also recognized David's insight into learning to wear a mask at work, where being openly gay or lesbian may attract disapproval or, worse, discriminatory practice. As David explained:

> ...as time goes on assumptions may be made. You start revealing less than you should about your life.

Working as a Church of England parish deaconess I struggled to 'come out', so I know the guarded steps Christina describes:

> *...careful steps and decisions, discomfiture sometimes, and alienation at other times, and being grateful when there was no need to be secretive, and increasingly becoming tired of it, of all those constraints.*

The public nature of civil partnership is described by the interview participants as particularly helpful in this context of overcoming secrecy, confusion and self-doubt. For Vanessa, this strengthened sense of self arrived with the declaration of vows that had a profoundly healing effect for her:

> *It wasn't until the ceremony that those words, that commitment out loud and, I don't know, I have never really spoken words that have meant or come alive so much! And, I don't know, it just affirmed our relationship and I was like, 'Yes, I am doing this wholeheartedly!'... I thought I was a person incapable of being loved by another person and Alice would soon realize I was a mistake. The ceremony changed that. It made me realize that Alice loved me unconditionally, for all my good and bad. It was the most beautiful and grounding experience.*

Stephen describes this pivotal point in his personal narrative as 'spine-tingling' and:

> *Almost like a closure of the previous chapter of my life, which was much more, um, a sort of chapter of uncertainty, the sense of the wilderness, in some sense... I struggled with a lot of issues which had to do with acceptance.*

Not all the research participants describe the action of performing the civil partnership rite itself as equally affirming of personal identity. Emma, who far earlier in her life had shared a full marriage-like act of commitment with her partner in another church, describes the conveyor-belt aspect of the register office rite:

> ...a bit like a cremation: as we were waiting to go in there was another
> happy couple coming out, as we were coming out there was another
> waiting to go in...just very quick.

Lucy, who added no content of her own choosing to the registration
ceremony, similarly describes it as having a less self-authenticating
effect:

> ...the actual rite was so, so secular, so kind of 'You are not allowed
> anything remotely religious'...

Yet for Emma and for Lucy, as for all the participants, other aspects
of arriving at a point of public recognition were described in
transformative terms, whether as a clarification of relationship status,
or as an act of justice, or as a challenge to taboo.

Clarification of the nature and status of the relationship

The second transformative effect was the beneficial effect of the civil
partnership rite in clarifying the nature of their intimate relationship.
The initial 'clarifying conversation' was, of course, with the partner,
where there is the discovery that the self is desired and desirable.
Rowan Williams (1996) suggests that such conversations are significant theologically on at least three levels. As we realize that we
are another's object of desire and joy, we are caught up in the life of
the Trinity where God desires us as if we were God, and in the life
of the Church whose purpose is to teach us by word and deed that
we are so desired by God. As each partner discovers themselves 'to be
seen in a certain way: as significant, as wanted' (p.59), they reflect the
very way God longs for us and desires us to know ourselves desirable.
One participant described how this significant conversation took
place below an ancient olive tree:

> And then that spring of 2011 we were on holiday and under an
> ancient olive tree he tapped me on the shoulder and said, you know?
> He didn't quite go down on one knee, but [laughs]...there was a sense
> of momentum, it was more than a conscious decision.

It was important to David, another participant, that this ultimate significance of each to the other was declared publicly:

> To me personally it is important because it is the ultimate form of a promise that I could make to my partner, and that he could make to me.

The public proclamation of promises itself effects change in the relationship. He and his partner each remember this personal and public commitment when they are experiencing difficulties and are consequently recalled to their resolve.

How we individuate within and from our family may be difficult where conversations about sexual orientation are fudged, feared or postponed under threat of strong disapproval where we most need to feel 'at home'. Lucy is clear that an important meaning of her civil partnership is clarity of relationship status within her family:

> What does it mean to me? Mainly the commitment to show to our families and friends... Families and friends matter because we kind of felt that maybe before it's like, 'Do we invite the other half?'

Clearly, not all conversations within families about civil partnership prove easy or welcomed. Five of the participants had no parent attending their celebration. Nevertheless, family conversations could prove fruitful in strengthening the sense of self, even where such conversations were not welcomed, as Stephen describes:

> I specifically travelled to see them a month before the civil partnership and I had one-on-one conversations with my family where I had to go not just one but two steps forward. I had to say to them (a) I am gay and (b) I am getting married to this man whom you have met. They knew that I lived with him, for all these years. But it was, you know, a big step forward.

Clarification may of course act as a two-edged sword. For some interviewees, the implicit discriminatory nature of the symbolic action caused anger. They expressed disgruntlement that civil partnership was itself at that time a symbolic 'outing' of the gay or lesbian person, since before 2019 heterosexual people were not offered civil partnership as a possibility. Eleven of the 13 participants mourned being unable to celebrate a civil marriage as a sign of equality with heterosexual people, having to accept civil partnership as 'the best they could do'. Nevertheless, the action acted as a hook on which to hang significant conversations.

David had not spoken to his mother about being gay, nor had it been wise to be open at work. The conversation with his mother caused her delight, while at work his identity with his partner became obvious and prevented further need to have individual conversations – conversations which in their intensity may not always be appropriate. Significantly, this idea was echoed in every interview. For some, living surrounded by respect and tolerance at work and at home, there was sheer relief at being able to celebrate an intimate relationship – described often as 'a blessing' – openly. Tom describes a celebration and party at church in the following way:

> I think 'blowing the roof off' almost changed from metaphor to reality at St Martin's, where I think there was a great sense of relief finally to be able to do this. We were among the first to hold a CP celebration there, and we invited all members of St Martin's to come, as well as our friends and family. We also then got the Crypt caterers to provide lunch after the service. At this party, we got our mothers to cut the cake. At the later garden party, it was our dads who did the same!

Effecting justice

All the interviewees understood civil partnership to bestow important legal rights in terms of equality with civil marriage. Tom understood it as the end of a long struggle for equality and does not seek the further step of marriage:

> Civil partnership gave us much appreciated equal legal rights, and outwardly a social recognition long sought for, fought for, and rightly ours.

Christina similarly underlines these practical consequences of expressing loving commitment through civil partnership:

> *Some of the important concomitants of loving commitment do involve things like financial resources, at the most important level housing and fundamental support for each other. And some other things, like taking mutual responsibility for care. So perhaps that's clearer than 'loving commitment', it involves a set of responsibilities of a practical kind, and the sharing of one's resources to support that. And that is important in the CP providing for the first time a legal framework for that, and legal protections for it.*

David places his civil partnership celebration in the light of the struggle for equality and of changing both the image and the reality of living in a gay relationship:

> *I see it also as important to me in my place in society. Um, for all sorts of reasons but, it's partly about a form of equal recognition. It's not the same as marriage quite, but it felt like that. And it's partly too to address some of the consequences of the way gay people have been treated unequally for so long. It's commonly thought and it's maybe right that statistically gay relationships don't last as long and aren't as stable as heterosexual ones. Now, I don't know if that's true, but if it is true then I am sure that one of the reasons for that is that gay relationships have not traditionally enjoyed the level of support given to straight couples. And I feel that civil partnership is just one way of redressing that inequality.*

Eleven participants state that seeking justice for gay and lesbian people is a strong motivation for taking this step.

Challenging taboo

My interest in investigating stories about a sensed presence of God in same-sex relationships came to a head with the experience of finding myself rigid with terror when I presented my first conference paper as an 'out' lesbian priest. In that presentation, I chose to disagree in public with the official teaching of the Church of England regarding sexual relationships for clergy, which is contained in *Issues in Human Sexuality: A Statement by the House of Bishops* (Church of England 1991): 'In our considered judgement the clergy cannot claim the liberty to enter into sexually active homophile relationships' (p.45). The event at which I spoke was small and friendly, welcoming only a hundred gay and lesbian Christians. It was held in my own home church, where I held tenure as the Rector. No press reporter was present. Yet I experienced catastrophic feelings about losing my job, being ridiculed, attracting punishment in some way. Seeking to understand this overwhelming sense of terror I read the work of Marilyn McCord Adams (1996) and of James Alison (2001, 2006, 2010). Reading their work was transformative for me, since it introduced me to the concept of taboo surrounding sexual behaviour and identities deemed disruptive by society or church. I began to understand why I felt so afraid.

In her work considering the apparent lack of justice towards gays and lesbians in the Church, Adams (1996) begins with the concept of 'taboo' as explored by the anthropologist Mary Douglas. In her book *Purity and Danger* (1966), Douglas had suggested that words like *purity* and *defilement* act as social metaphors, used to build evaluative systems that protect social definitions and boundaries. Douglas's hypothesis was that societies under threat tend to develop elaborate rules surrounding purity and pollution. Because sexual behaviour is so charged with energy and lies at the heart of self-and-other definition, and because sexual relationships will carry the family, tribe and race into a strong or weak future, it is an easy target for the strongest of these rules – the rule of taboo. Taboo gains strength by rendering absolutely unthinkable any behaviour that threatens to undermine social foundations, and gains further power by being understood to be the will of a family, tribal or national god.

Adams (1996) understands the continuing power of the taboo against homosexual behaviour, despite its being weakened considerably in modern secular society, to lie in three areas. First, there is the threat contained within a text considered sacred (see Chapter 6) to undermine the mental health and identity formation of the gay or lesbian person, especially if they are isolated by their youth or lack of supportive social contacts. Taboo resists rational thought and excludes an individual not through any willed behaviour of their own but simply by their very being. Second, the very insistence on the irrational whereby taboos maintain power also permits irrationally cruel and abusive behaviour to be perpetrated against the perceived taboo bearers. Third, while there are signs of a decreased institutionalization of homophobic attitudes and taboos, stubborn resistance to change also persists, with accompanying outbursts of homophobic bullying and violence.

Eleven of the 13 research participants had experienced fear of breaking a taboo in knowing and expressing themselves as gay or lesbian in the context of belonging to family, school, colleagues or church. Christina describes how unthinkable it would be to family and church to declare herself lesbian:

> Homosexuality was utterly taboo, in the sense at any rate of being utterly rendered invisible and unacceptable, um, and not to be acknowledged or talked about. Yes, so, taboo has notions of that and of being unclean and defiling and that was implicit in the culture in which I grew up and sinful... I think all that was very strong.

Sue describes turning away from training in a church-affiliated institution after hearing church members give offensive descriptions of gay and lesbian people:

> Some of the things people said were hideous, not Christian, horrible and hateful, and I thought, 'I can't do this'.

Stephen indicates how being silent about gay identity within the family caused him distressing anxiety:

> The relationship with my family has always been a problem. The two-faced nature of it as well, because my family and parents live in another country and I would always travel twice a year to see them and at that point I would have to be their straight son...that sort of sense of two-faced existence really bothered me. I had nightmares for several years actually, really awful nightmares. So, this all went away when I sort of opened myself to them.

The theologian James Alison, resonating with Douglas's analysis, understands how this sense of terror fuelled the silence of his boyhood as a gay child:

> Sheer panic engulfed me… My awareness, as a nine-year-old, that I was completely lost and alone in a dangerous and hostile world, in which the thing that I most wanted – the love of another boy and to be with him forever – was not only impossible but utterly reprobate and an abomination. (2010, p.188)

Alison (2010) investigated further the power and importance of taboo in holding threatened cultures together and in banishing or destroying victims who are under its ban. What is particularly significant in his work for practical theology is both that he understands the overturning of taboo to be part of the essential Christ event and that he considers himself to be writing from within the story (pp.186–208). He is a gay theologian who writes for all people who find themselves in a place of annihilating taboo (pp.230–249). His mentor is the French ethnologist René Girard, and it is impossible to understand Alison without comprehending what Girard himself wrote about taboo, the scapegoat mechanism and the Christ figure of the Gospels.

In the views of both Girard and Alison, Jesus attempted to convert Israel away from a social and religious ethic, which rested on taboo and the punishment of the scapegoat, towards a love ethic. When he fails in this task of persuasion, he offers himself as an innocent victim to stem the violence he has caused and to help his followers see through the lie behind the device – it is innocent victims who are killed when this mechanism is used to create social and political harmony. Peter the Apostle demonstrates his understanding of what Jesus has done in his interpretation of his dream about clean and unclean foods in Acts 10. Here, Alison suggests, a 'post-taboo religion' is formed, for those with eyes to see. Peter has understood that that not only are no foods under taboo but there is no longer a group of people standing against another group in a superior position with God. No people by virtue of their birth or their behaviour are unclean or outside or inferior. From now on certain strands of Christian thinking will continue to use taboo to exclude whoever is perceived to be the next necessary victim, while other strands will work for liberation and the demolition of taboos. Girard and Alison both believe that the Church is likely to perpetuate the scapegoat mechanism, victimizing people under taboo, because it likes to set up clear categories of good and bad human behaviour and to identify clear 'enemies'. But at the same time other groups within it, and increasingly in secular society, will understand the moral imperative to stand beside victims of human persecution in all its forms.

As Girard suggested of this and every other cultural upheaval, people outside the power of conservative religious institutions step freely into places of taboo and show them to be utterly survivable (Girard 2001). They begin to destabilize the taboo.

Christina describes this destabilization process in her own life and the role of civil partnership in this ongoing process. She spoke of her first important loving, sexual encounter which broke through this sense of taboo as:

> an explosion of recognition, which burst through that blanket covering which I think I had thrown over that unacceptable set of longings and desires. Feeling both ecstatic and self-doubting at the same time.

Gradually over the years, as another relationship flowered, the inner sense of self-doubt disappeared. Yet Christina added that an important meaning for her in the rite of civil partnership was, nevertheless, validation:

> What changed with the civil partnership was not so much my internal position as my sense of a more public, civic, social foundation.

Christina and her partner held a large, joyous celebration of civil partnership, with a hundred people including many generations of family members attending both registration and the following party. She is articulate about both the happiness she felt and the reasons why:

> I felt extremely happy throughout the process... Confirmation of value is probably what I think I mean by validation. So the self-doubt and fear in the very earliest stages meant that I was not a person of value

> and, at the very first, in some fundamental way, sinful, because that
> was my very first experience of my question about what this meant.
> And that probably planted a seed about my own self-worth as a full
> human being, which certainly changed over time and diminished, but I
> experienced the civil partnership and its public setting with friends and
> family and the wider society and the legal system which is our civil
> society as recognition and confirmation of the value of myself in the
> context of this relationship.

Christina is clear that homophobic attitudes have not been completely
overcome:

> I suppose the most obvious difficulty was the whole question of how
> open or secretive to be in the vast range of circumstances in which one
> found oneself. That's not completely gone even to this day because you
> can never be completely confident that you will be accepted, whether
> in this country and certainly sometimes abroad.

It is in this context of living under a taboo that the external validation
of long-term committed same-sex relationships in public rites of
celebration is particularly significant for society and for the Church.
But while the Church is quick in its formal statements to condemn
all forms of homophobic bullying and oppression, the attitudes that
fuel such violence are supported by the religious taboo surrounding
homosexuality. This research shows that such taboos begin to be
eroded where homosexual relationships, far from being condemned,
are openly celebrated and given legal status.

The Church's continuing failure to welcome such celebrations,
and to provide authorized liturgies to support their celebration,
is particularly difficult to tolerate as there is evidence of LGBTQ
Christians using the resources of faith to support their decision to
enter civil partnerships, and to create a moral framework around both
rite and relationship. Participants in this research turn to the Bible, to
Church tradition, and to reason, to test and resource the strength and
direction of their relationship and life of faith. With regard to each
resource I attended in my analysis both to ideas that gave impetus

to registration as civil partners, and to ideas that created a moral framework around both rite and relationship.

Using the resources of faith
The use of the Bible

In terms of the use of the Bible there are two strands of thought that supported the impulse to enter a civil partnership. The first, described by Lucy, concerns the use of biblical theology and imagery to support 'coming out', particularly to self. Lucy, like many other participants, decided that she had been created gay by God, and so could accept and forgive herself for this, after a period of 'trying not to be'. She understands herself to have been found by God, like the prodigal son (Luke 15:11–32) and, being found, is able to be both gay and faithful to God.

A second impulse to enter a civil partnership is linked with the biblical theme of God's harvest and Eucharistic abundance. Christina used these lines from U.A. Fanthorpe's (1987) poem '7301' in her civil partnership celebration, to hint at this sense of shared abundance:

I hold them crammed in my arms, colossal crops
Of shining tomorrows that may never happen,
But may they!

The abundance is to be shared as witness to others of possibilities for their lives. David, referring to Matthew 5:15, understood the religious celebration of the rite as 'not hiding our light under a bushel basket'.

There was also evidence of biblical theology creating a framework of meaning for the relationship itself. Seven interviewees emphasized the vital importance of living forgiveness in their relationship; four participants sensed guidance by the Holy Spirit, while another's image of his relationship as a 'rare and beautiful bird' resonates with this theme, as in Genesis 1:2 the Spirit of God broods like a bird over the face of the waters. Six participants understand themselves called to a new and uncertain way of life, as were the disciples by Jesus, and to have entered a covenant relationship of promise with their partner and with God.

What is particularly striking is affectionate mention by ten research participants of the stories of Ruth and Naomi (Ruth 1:16). These figures, who strike out on unusual and difficult life journeys in loyal support of each other, act as models of loyalty, faithfulness in journey, bonding outside the expected norms of behaviour and willingness to journey into the unknown, entering each other's 'strange' family. The story is utterly new to Matthew, who is delighted when his partner both introduces it to him and re-writes it as vows to use in the civil partnership registration rite where the Bible story was of course refused:

> My partner gave that reading to me. I didn't want the readings which were in my mind which were more clichéd, and Ruth and Naomi were the most authentic, the most real and tangible...at the town hall we squeezed in Ruth and Naomi by saying the words to each other.

Emma jokes that she and her family remind each other of this story when there is a difficult family visit to make to in-laws, while Anne gives a lesbian interpretation of the story:

> 'Your people shall be my people', you know the whole thing about that feels to me like the inclusion of being part of a community of lesbians, if you like... I get a lot of strength from being with other couples who are lesbians too, because you just relax and be ourselves. It's never quite that way with straight couples.

The Bible offered support for understanding 'the good' of both the rite and the relationship of civil partnership to 11 participants. For one participant, there is no evidence of it having a supportive role. On the contrary, he has rejected it and Christianity, finding spiritual freedom and inspiration:

> ...not dwelling in the past, or in a fantasy future, and in shedding the chains of an obsession with sin and an all-demanding, never-satisfied 'God'.

The use of Church tradition

Research participants make rich use of the resources of theology and Church tradition to form and support their views. They turn, first, to an understanding of the meaning and experience of the love of God. Eight participants suggested that an understanding of the love of God, whether to be enjoyed or to be shared with others, had been a creative impulse in leading them to enter a civil partnership. Both Vanessa and Lucy, the youngest participants, stated that it was understanding this divine love for them that had prepared them to be able to freely love another. Learning about that love of God in the theology and community life of St Martin's had been immensely helpful to Vanessa:

> I was brought up a Catholic and I was told that I couldn't be gay and that I wasn't accepted in the Church and I kind of left. I left my faith behind for quite some time. And then I have been going to St Martin-in-the-Fields for four to five years now and, opening up that door again to God, it was refreshing because, like I said at the beginning, I allowed myself to be fully loved by God, every aspect of myself, and also loving back. And that kind of taught me how to do that. And then I could put that in place with Alice. It made me more loving as a person.

Emma and her partner had enjoyed a service of celebration of their relationship, which Emma understood to be a marriage service, very many years before civil partnership became a possibility. For her, her new awareness of the love of God in the community of the local church was a vital impetus towards taking this step:

> ...taking the step also influenced my faith. The decision to commit came first, or rather the love came first, then came the decision to commit. And then the opportunity to express that in a religious setting came alongside a growing spirituality in me. And so the opportunity to weave my life with my partner's life and God in one big ceremony, um, it cemented me into a church community, where I was really very happy for the next several years.

Second, almost all participants had drawn on patterns of enduring marriage to shape their own hopes for the future of their relationship. While this theme will be studied more closely in Chapter 5, here it is useful to notice Christina's description of the impetus for civil partnership:

> I think that, culturally, commitment and committed relationships belong to where I come from in terms of a certain kind of upbringing and religious context. And this commitment is part of that. Commitment is probably rather deeply imbued in me and could be linked to a strong underpinning, a Christian set of values.

In terms of an ethical framework for the relationship, the resources of Church tradition also proved to be a rich seam for participants to mine. This tradition will be examined further in terms of a theology of liberation in Chapter 3, where challenging taboo is itself a theological position, and in terms of the theology of marriage in Chapter 5, where the good of monogamy is examined.

Finally, given that this research sample consists of Church congregation members, it is unsurprising that Church belonging and traditional expressions of faith – prayer, worship, Bible study, reading theology, friendship with Church members – all appear as vital elements of Church tradition on which participants draw for sustenance in ethical decision making about their partnership. Lillian speaks movingly of the way Church friends have helped her and her partner pastorally:

> We have had a lot of lovely little reminders from that day, from quite significant people, when we got into difficulties or when we have had, you know, just stress, from life and work and relationships and family – things that put a strain on our relationship.

Conversely, two interviewees are repelled by the negative critical tone of recurring official Church of England statements about homosexuality, civil partnership and gay marriage. Both no longer belong to Church as members and demonstrate sorrow and rage at the Church's official teaching. Tom remonstrates:

> I think my experience of civil partnership, and celebrating that partly within a church, has only subsequently made me more aware of just how distanced institutionalized 'faiths' have become from the realities of human life and progress. It is an abiding shame to me that it is now society challenging the Church to catch up, rather than the other way around. To me, it is only so much cant that asserts that the Church must hold on to 'traditional teaching' – who has the right to say, absolutely, what on earth that is?

Emma is brought near to tears in the interview by a corresponding sense of exclusion that official Church teaching has engendered for her:

> I think that I kept on, like a sort of domestic violence thing, I kept giving the Church another chance. You know the sort of thing, there are really nice people in the Church. The churchwarden in X town was a really lovely woman, a good friend, and she was hurt that we didn't go to church. Sometimes I think I would go to church to please her. But it left me just numb inside.

For 11 research participants, the love of God, belonging to Church, the example of enduring marriage, and the traditional practices of faith prove a rich wealth of resource in their journey away from lack of self-worth and into civil partnership. For two participants, the experience of continued rejection by Church members and ministers, and official Church statements voicing disapproval of gay and lesbian relationships, have led them to seek nurturing spiritual paths outside the traditions of the Church.

The use of reason

What are the normative stories which persuaded participants that to enter their relationships of civil partnership was a moral 'good'? I detected two strong themes in my analysis of the transcripts. The first is a set of assumptions about what constitutes a fulfilling relationship, which the sociologist Giddens (1992, pp.13–16) interprets as part of the 'transformation of intimacy' detectable in the culture of today.

The second is an enjoyment of belonging within the history of gay liberation.

Ted, Matthew, Susan, Lillian and Lucy use very different language to describe what helps their relationships flourish. Ted uses the language of co-counselling, a movement in which he shares with his partner:

> I think that in practising commitment to my partner I gain the skill of being able to pay attention, make sacrifices when necessary, remember to be happy, all these things. So, through the doing, through the everyday living, and remembering to do it that I'll achieve something that makes me happy ultimately and him too.

Matthew uses the language of growing in authenticity. Susan uses the language of adopting complementary roles that suit their personalities, both at home and in social interactions. Lucy suspects that her partnership is unusual in the way both she and Sarah focus on the care of their child but says, simply, 'It works for us.' What these and other participants hold in common is that they all state that they have decided what they consider to be the ingredients for human happiness in relationship, and check from time to time that those ingredients still hold. Stephen illustrates this listing and checking:

> There is equality in respecting each other's wishes, and our tastes. So, you know, I like modern dance and we went to a ballet last night, that my partner just completely dissed from minute one, which was incredibly disappointing,

The sociologist Anthony Giddens (1991, 1992) identifies modern cultural influences upon and shapes within intimate adult relationships. He writes of the emergence in our culture of the idea of the 'pure relationship', where the partners, set free from ties of family and local tradition, decide for themselves what gives them a sense of intense, communicative interdependence and of self-completion through the difference of the other (1992, pp.49–64). Stephen describes this 'unmoored' meeting and intensity of hope in the other:

> I would say that, you know, when I met my partner, randomly at a club
> as you know, on, um, the day before New Year's Eve, we hit it off straight
> away. And we were very into each other from the beginning and saw
> each other on a daily basis and there was that sort of great enthusiasm
> and the anxiety. So there was this sort of first six months of sleeplessness
> because you were excited about what was happening in your life and
> you had this gut feeling that 'this is it'. Somehow this relationship that
> you have been waiting for has now materialized.

Lillian is clear that equality of power is an important part of mutuality,
and that is not always easy to achieve:

> One of the things that was really, really significant is that my partner
> is a boss type, and I am a helper type. [Balancing power is] one of the
> things which is really difficult for us in nearly twenty years...

As Giddens suggests, high degrees of openness and honesty are
expected in a successful relationship. Again, Stephen says:

> ...what really brought it to a head, the idea that we would do this
> commitment of civil partnership, was my partner not acknowledging to
> third parties in a couple of incidents, somebody at work, that we were
> a couple, or that he was in a gay relationship because he didn't want
> that to come out. And I said, 'I'm in a different space from you, I'm
> completely open about this. You have got to deal with this, in the most
> open and honest way.'

The language of the transformation of intimacy is present here in the
degree to which research participants are seeking personal fulfilment
in intensity of feelings, the communication of shared values, and
democracy in decision making.

Yet there are two striking differences between Giddens's
understanding of intimate relationships and those represented in
this research. Giddens (1992, p.137) suggests that moderns seek
self-fulfilment in relationship as a primary good, and that once self-
fulfilment in the other is not forthcoming, the relationship is over and

the next is sought. In contrast, all the participants interviewed for this research study seek lifelong intimacy. Here David states:

> And civil partnership...is I think a great thing because it's a sort of steady reminder of the permanence of what we have undertaken. And it's always there, um, irrespective of the trials and tribulations of our relationship.

This emphasis on lifelong commitment is a major consideration in what creates a moral good in relationship for all 13 participants.

There is also no space in Giddens's description of the pure relationship for Matthew and others' vision of decreased self-centredness in relationship and for the moral good of growing in self-giving. Matthew insists:

> If I am not transformed by the relationship, then I know that this is not a true relationship...transformed in the direction of self-giving... The transformation is the sign and my transformation as a Christian and my transformation as a person outside the Church, which again in my mind they are the same. Noticing this transformation is what I hold on to is, if there is a question like 'Are you really in a healthy relationship?' just go to that.

This research suggests that the participants are influenced by the changing cultural norms for intimate relationships, which Giddens studies and describes. However, they alter, change and discard those norms where they conflict with other influences gained from the Christian tradition like those of lifelong monogamy, faithfulness and self-giving to partner and wider world.

Another story that research participants share is that of enjoying the fruits of gay liberation and increased tolerance towards gay and lesbian people in secular society. The three youngest women have known no discrimination against them in their friendship groups. Emma states, of tolerance towards her as a student in the 1990s:

> I was a student and out so didn't have any issues around that.

And Lucy describes how quickly the choice to enter a civil partnership became a non-controversial issue:

> Yes. Yes, it hadn't really crossed my mi... I guess it must have done because people that I had known before had been in a civil partnership.

Anne, by contrast, some years older, was aware of taking the slow steps towards legal recognition of her relationship with her partner:

> ...when we got together, we very quickly did all the legal stuff so wills, and enduring powers of attorney and all that, we did that anyway. And we wanted to have some formal recognition of our relationship. So, when Ken Livingstone did the London thing, when he registered partnerships, we went and did that...and then as soon as civil partnerships became available, we thought that we would do that too.

The two youngest male participants had no sense of taking tolerance of sexual orientation and civil partnership for granted, since they had both grown up in less liberal cultures. They show a sense of liberation more in common with Tom, an older participant who summarizes the struggle which had taken place:

> Civil partnership gave us much appreciated equal legal rights, and outwardly a social recognition long sought for, fought for, and rightly ours.

Ted understood himself to be part of the struggle for gay liberation in the Catholic Church of the United States, and to stand on the shoulders of heroes in that movement such as Robert Goss:

> When I was 21 or so, I knew Bob Goss – do you know him? Robert Goss? He wrote Jesus Acted Up: A Gay and Lesbian Manifesto – soon after he wrote the book. He is a former Jesuit and he was married religiously, because it wasn't possible civilly, to a Jesuit novice. And he said that he and Frank were a Jesuit community of two.

While using very different language, all research participants suggest how the paths through being open about their relationships and civil partnership are steps to increase justice for gay and lesbian people suffering discrimination. By now I had established that the public act of civil partnership had not merely contained words about faithfulness in relationship, but also effected positive changes in the inner and outer life of partners: changes in self-belief, clearer relationships with families, friends, work colleagues and church, greater justice in society, and steps in the erosion of dangerous taboo. I had also begun to understand that LGBTQ Christians see meanings of God in both rite and relationship, as Sue hints here:

> It sounds a bit pretentious but you know a snapshot of the Divine, you know that whole thing about honesty and truth and openness and kindness and love, you know things in Corinthians about what love is, they are all pictures of God, aren't they? So...in that sense the relationship does have elements of... good elements in it, which are from God.

From my analysis I concluded that 12 of the 13 research participants understand their relationships to both point to and participate in God. I began to think about the sacramental nature of civil partnership:

The sacramental nature of civil partnership

In his sermon 'Is there a Christian sexual ethic?', Rowan Williams links our understanding of the sacraments with the theology of the Incarnation:

> The Gospel is about a man who made his entire life a sign that speaks of God and who left to his followers the promise that they too could *be* signs of God and *make* signs of God because of him. (1994, p.164)

Williams continues in this sermon to explore the meaning of Christ as sacrament, and the potentiality for our sexual nature to consequently show 'meanings' of God:

Jesus is himself the first and greatest sacrament, and he creates the possibility of things and persons, acts and places being in some way sacramental in the light of what he has done. … Now, if my life can communicate the 'meanings' of God, this must mean that my sexuality too can be sacramental; it can speak of mercy, faithfulness, transfiguration and hope. (1994, p.164)

Participants speak of recognizing these qualities in their relationships. In her partner, Vanessa sees Christ wearing a drawn-on moustache for mercy's sake:

> I do see Christ in Alice every day, which makes me smile. There have been times when I have got ill, and Alice has stopped work to look after me. She didn't know if I was going to get better or not. She kept faith that I was going to get better. I think she felt helpless, like she couldn't do anything, but, you know, she would still go into the bathroom and draw a moustache on her face. And I would turn around to talk to her and see this moustache on her face and it would make me laugh. Those small things would lighten up the day. Alice does that all the time.

Emma's life has been transformed by the faithfulness that exists between herself and her partner:

> You know, we have been through periods of calm and periods of turbulence of course, but I have never doubted the…there have been times when we have been separately quite unhappy, but I have never doubted that the relationship would survive. Even when there has been conflict between us, that's like the surface turbulence but the deep stuff is really, I feel, very secure.

Matthew does not speak of transfiguration but of 'transformation in the direction of self-giving'. David speaks of 'showing God's glory' known in the shared love between him and his partner. Sue speaks of 'becoming more Christ-like' because she is securely loved. Vanessa, perhaps most strongly among the participants because she is a painter, hints at the 'radiant cloud' or 'glory' of God's presence in the Transfiguration known in her relationship by her use of the language of the 'sublime', 'infinity', 'limitless depth'. She illustrates her descriptions by use of Mark Rothko's painting 'Light, Earth and Blue'[1] to illustrate her feelings of being overawed by the depth of her relationship:

> Because of the blue he uses is best to express that sense of infinity, limitless depth, maybe because of our associations with nature. The sky is blue, and seems to be limitless, and so is the ocean. And that's how I see – also I think there is a sense of the sublime in this painting and it's that kind of unknown territory which is kind of scary but exciting at the same time. That's how I see my relationship with Alice because our love grows every day, stronger and stronger.

When asked what beliefs undergird his relationship of commitment to his partner, Stephen includes the word *hope* and the comfort based in shared belief in Christ:

> Love, mutual respect, self-sacrifice, and also hope. Um, commitment, dedication, and you know I think that that all is derived from [our Christian faith], and I take great comfort from the fact that all these are reciprocated I think, because largely we are, we have a Christian belief system. We believe in Christ and I think that I don't have a reason to doubt any of these things because that's what fundamentally he believes.

Rowan Williams suggests that homosexual relationships may be sacramental signs of God's presence, which participate in the 'meanings' of God since they reflect and participate in, as heterosexual relationships do, the very desire of God for us. This mutual joy and delight in the other, including the other who is God, is glimpsed in the research evidence.

The participants show how in many ways, as the American feminist theologian Sallie McFague suggests in her work on parables and the language of metaphor, 'the transcendent comes to ordinary

---

1   www.artnet.com/artists/mark-rothko/light-earth-and-blue-2vUFO0r
     ZxKoz1LKf0ncy4g2

reality and disrupts it (1975, p.xv). Yet, what is easily overlooked about the ordinary reality described in this research is that it is the reality of lesbian and gay lives. The theology that has sprung from their particular experience is, in my view, queer theology. It resists and interrogates heteronormativity, the notion that heterosexuality is the best way forwards for all individuals, all societies, all expressions of religious faith. As queer theology it adds two deeper dimensions of Christian understanding to what I mean by the 'sacramental quality' of these rites and relationships. For the Christ of queer theology is both excluded and disruptive. This queer Christ is known both in the pain and longing of these lives, as well as in their fulfilment and joy.

Queer theology reminds us that Jesus is a figure of human exclusion. Matthew, one of the interviewees, understanding this exclusion, wished to represent the Christ who brings division in this reading from the Gospel of Matthew at his church celebration, yet was prevented from doing so by the priest celebrating the service:

> Do not suppose that I had come to bring peace to the earth: it is not peace I have come to bring, but a sword. For I have come to set son against father, daughter against mother, daughter-in-law against mother-in-law; a person's enemies will be the members of his own household. (Matthew 10:34)

There are sorrowful stories here of feeling excluded by the Church. One participant, Lillian, who worked in a faith school, did not feel she could tell her staff colleagues that in her eyes she had been married during the summer vacation:

> *I thought, I bet no other straight woman in the world would have got married over the summer and not feel able to tell anyone about it, and say, 'I had a nice summer, thank you.' I've got wedding pictures, in my dress and things, and didn't say anything.*

Seven participants excluded themselves from church attendance for several years over Church attitudes towards homosexuality. One had given up religious faith long before the period of this research began, and one, Emma, has left since. She states:

> *We moved...and the village church was, the priest there was homophobic and, you know, in that terribly nice way and, you know, 'Nothing personal, I just don't think that...' Yeah, right. So, we didn't go to church very much. And around that time, I realized that it wasn't bothering me as much as I thought it should. I just put up some shutters, I was terribly hurt.*

The presence of narratives of exclusion, completely entangled with stories of celebration, remind us of the God in Christ, who identified himself with the excluded and was himself cast out of the city. The inclusive meaning of God's holiness is lived in these accounts, which the queer theologian Marcella Althaus-Reid, whose work will figure largely in Chapters 3 and 4, calls 'testimonies of real lives in rebellious modes of love, pleasure and suffering' (2004, p.152). She writes of a 'Queer sense of holiness' springing from the God known in this excluded Christ: 'A Queer sense of holiness goes beyond exclusion, nurtured from the solidarity of a God identified as an excluded among excluded' (p.152). If these relationships possess a sacramental quality, the Christ who is known here is precisely that 'crucified and risen victim' who, James Alison suggests, sets us free to move beyond our own sense of triumphalism in relationship, in order to reach out to other excluded ones:

> It is a question of moving human desire out of a pattern of relating to others from rivalry, a relationship based on death, to a relationship based on a pacific imitation of Jesus, leading to a relationship with others of gratuity, service. (1993, p.56)

Queer theology also helps us identify another sacramental quality in these narratives, for they are saturated with a sense of God's disruptive future breaking into time. Christina understands Jesus as a figure who disrupts punitive patterns of human correction and rejection. At this point in her interview with me she has been handed a picture famously called 'The Woman Caught in Adultery', and reacts like this:

> *I think that this is the story [John 8:1–11] where the people and the religious authorities are singling out an individual for brutal and*

> *harsh treatment because of something in her life we don't know much about, but a relationship of some kind. And Jesus's careful and effective challenging of those assumptions of the religious authority and replacing that with an expression of love, containment, protection. This resonates with me as that sense that God challenges those ways in which we as human beings enslave each other and entrap each other in rigid patterns of rejection. Um, and that instead God opens that up with love. And that fits for me as an expression of what has happened around the civil partnership.*

For almost all participants, the future life of God has broken into their life in the form of radical forgiveness, as Sue describes:

> *This is the first relationship I have ever had in which I don't have any fear about doing things wrong. That's not to say that I don't do anything wrong, I mess up. But I think we bring out the best in each other, so I don't feel so fearful and I don't get things wrong so much and it's a kind of cyclical thing.*

It has broken in, in beauty and abundance, as David states:

> *These are images of human beauty, and are all God given, and again beauty and what is God given are to me at the heart of my relationship... Can I talk about Jesus turning the water into wine? It is for me an example of a story which epitomizes...making the most of our blessings. Jesus wanted us to have a good time! I firmly believe that! That doesn't mean having a good time at the expense of others. It just means making the most of what you have got in a way that works well. And Jesus was all for that.*

The eschatological nature of such sacramental presence is shown in the ways such relationships point to God's future of justice for all who know themselves to be oppressed. Ted used his church service of thanksgiving for civil partnership to show the Church 'where God wants the world to be'. It is shown in an awareness among the participants of that future God acting now to bring people into communion with each other and with God. The in-breaking and more just future of God is described in 'How Can I Keep From Singing?' (Lowry 1869), a song that Christina chose for her civil partnership celebration:

> *My life goes on in endless song*
> *Above earth's lamentations,*
> *I hear the real, though far-off hymn*
> *That hails a new creation.*
>
> *Through all the tumult and the strife*
> *I hear its music ringing.*
> *It sounds an echo in my soul,*
> *How can I keep from singing?*
>
> *While though the tempest loudly roars,*
> *I hear the truth, it liveth.*
> *And though the darkness 'round me close,*
> *Songs in the night it giveth.*

Conclusion

In response to the government consultation on the future of civil partnership following the Marriage (Same Sex Couples) Act, the Church of England found greater approval for civil partnership (Church of England 2014), laying greater emphasis on its usefulness as a social and legal framework for the recognition of same-sex partnerships. Nevertheless, the use of Church of England buildings as places of registration remained denied; nor was there to be written an authorized liturgy of blessing or thanksgiving following civil partnership. Despite the sense of grudging approval offered for the right ordering of same-sex relationships legally and financially, these further prohibitions underline the sense that civil partnership is not to be celebrated socially and liturgically as the full joining of persons, body, soul and spirit.

The queer theologian Althaus-Reid suggests that 'God comes out from heterosexual theology when the voices from sexual dissidents speak out to the churches' (2004, p.176). I close this chapter with the suggestion that relationships of civil partnership have a sacramental quality, and that I begin to understand rites of civil partnership as, in my own words, 'Coming out Ceremonies for God'. For in these relationships the desire of God for human beings is reflected in the desire participants feel for their partner, while the mercy, faithfulness, transfiguration and hope of God are experienced in the flesh of these research participants' everyday lives. These justice-seeking, future-orientated queer Christian narratives are resonant not with of a lack of holiness – let alone blasphemy – but with the story of a marginalized, crucified Christ who allows himself to be outpoured, misunderstood and ridiculed in love, yet whose love is a 'God-send', healing human life of loneliness, saving human life from alienation. This should be cause for Christian celebration.

These are powerful rites, effecting change for the good in individuals and their communities. These are sacramental rites, bearing witness to a God who speaks and acts in outsider places. The Christians participating in this research find their relationships compatible with faith, producing spiritual growth, and increasing their capacity to do justly and to love mercy. It is time for the Church to acknowledge what is already happening in queer lives, and to rejoice.

Chapter 3

ESCAPE FROM WILDERNESS

Stephen, a research participant, understands one meaning of his civil partnership to be an exodus from a place of oppression. He describes it like this:

> I feel that I have had in my life a sort of persecution, perhaps not quite like the Israelites had with the Egyptians following them, but I have had a sense of persecution in the sense that I was running away from a lot, from my previous life, from my family, from a culture of constraint and prejudice, to a life where I could be, where I could feel at home.

Civil partnership is for him the sense of arriving home:

> It means a sense of security, safety, a sense of completion, and a sort of, almost like a closure of the previous chapter of my life, which was much more a sort of chapter of uncertainty, the sense of the wilderness, in some sense.

Samuel Wells, writing about the biblical book of Exodus, suggests how here, and at every stage of Old Testament history, salvation emerges from setback and suffering, as I find occurring in many participants' narratives (2015, p.58). Faith in God motivated Stephen and his partner to enter a civil partnership:

> I would say it was probably the number one factor.

And faith continues to act as a building block for the relationship:

> *The sort of seeking guidance, seeking peace, seeking hope again, um, praying together, that is a very important building block of our relationship.*

He is also clear about the liberating role of Church in the celebration of his civil partnership in a service of prayer and dedication:

> *It helps break through the taboo – the fact that someone is willing to go along with it, willing to believe that this can be done. You know, that is such a great impetus. It was almost like we fell in love all over again – with each other, and then with the Church...*

David, whose childhood and early adulthood was less painful than that of Stephen, nevertheless speaks of a return from exile. He focuses on the biblical language of God leading a way home for those returning from Babylon to Jerusalem to rebuild their city, as he reflects on the story of return found in the biblical book of Ezra:

> *I do think that the return from exile story is one which metaphorically matters because it was the story of both what was offered to those returning, the promise of freedom in God, but also the responsibility that they held to make the most of what was given to them through that return from exile.*

Christina, by contrast, links the language of exodus, of being freed from oppression, with being part of a wide secular liberation movement:

> *...the exodus from slavery in Egypt. There is a liberation movement which has been involving gay people in the latter part of the 20th century and the early part of the 21st century in this part of the world, a liberation struggle going on in other parts too. Only today coming home from work I read about an African man coming out as gay, a well-known author. There is a liberation story which we are just so fortunate to be part of.*

She describes the way this movement for liberation has affected her life:

> *The period during which I have lived knowing myself as lesbian dates from 1981 to 2014 – during that period society in the UK has made the most immense changes. Despite some preliminary positive stirrings we then had the AIDS crisis, and a lot of negative taboo aspects in relation to that, and then Section 28 and the challenges of that, and then the suggestion that gay people were in some way damaging to families and family life and children. And really through the 90s and especially since 2000 a hugely more positive public narrative about gay people. Civil partnership represented both the struggle for equality led by key groups, but also the public shift and recognition. So those changes in society also obviously affected me.*

James Alison suggests that changes in society such as gay liberation may be understood as signs of the Kingdom of God working in the midst of our humanity. Alison writes:

> The whole wave of changes in society which 'just happen' and which are bigger and more powerful than any of us, are not simply entirely evil and corrupt, but are part of what enables us to be brought into being, which is in itself something good. (2007, p.55)

In Christina's account there is a breaking down of the barriers between Church and world, sacred and secular history, a destruction of binary thinking, which is one aspect of queer theology. The queer theologian Stone suggests: 'Perhaps the biblical stories that queer readers need to focus upon are not…stories that constitute religious identities in polarised terms or make absolute distinctions between insiders and outsiders' (2004, p.132). Rather, 'We may need to commit ourselves instead to the task of dissolving those very boundaries between "inside" and "outside"' (p.134).

Varieties of wilderness

Research participants understand the liberation brought about by their relationships of civil partnership in four broad ways. Seven speak of escape from a wilderness of alienation within the self. Eleven speak of knowing conflict within their family. Others suffer a sense of alienation in the surrounding society, including 11 who have experienced the threat of violence. A shocking but significant finding is that three research participants have known actual violence, with two also reporting accounts of sexual abuse, and six have known homophobic bullying. In spiritual terms nine participants report having known a sense of alienation from God.

A wilderness within the self

Lillian describes the wilderness of alienation caused by internalized homophobia, which was familiar to seven research participants:

> Everything negative I've experienced about being gay-ish is because I've taken all this time to come to terms with my fears. If I think someone is looking at us funnily on the train, for example, and we're holding hands, I feel it's unsafe and I let go. So, I do have some anxieties and fears but it's because of both real and imagined homophobia.

She continues:

> I found everything difficult! I didn't like being different. I didn't like having to keep my relationships closeted. School, you know I always taught in Church of England schools because you know, it's funny, but I was drawn to and repelled by them. The one time I tried to go somewhere else I hated it and was bullied for being gay, at school by the other staff, and had a horrible time.

She experiences calm in her relationship of 23 years with her partner, whom she knows as a gift from God:

> But in the God I know in my marriage there is something very holding about that... And when I see or hear such awful things as happen – like human trafficking – on the streets of London and think how can there be a God? Then I think, hang on, my partner is so lovely, therefore there

> *must be a God, because why would I have been sent this lovely person to live with, and be with, and love?*

A wilderness within the family

Eleven participants have known difficulties within their family of origin caused by their identity as gay or lesbian. David eloquently describes such difficulties:

> *I remember having an argument with my father when I must have been about 15 or something and he must have just heard something in what I had said and he said, 'Don't turn gay on me, please.' I didn't say anything, but it's always lived with me ever since.*

For some, these difficulties have been relatively short lived, but for six others a sense of estrangement remains. Here Stephen speaks of the anguish caused by trying to appear heterosexual at home:

> *It creates a dislocation and a sense of anxiety, so I had various night-mares always featuring my mother, for several years, really awful nightmares. So, this all went away when I sort of opened myself to them.*

While long-standing difficulties diminished very slowly in his family of origin, Stephen experienced at the religious celebration of his civil partnership the God who is a shield over his new family. This new family is created both by his joining the welcoming family of his partner, and also by building a family of his own, with friends and their children living together with him and his partner in one shared home:

> *I felt...a shield almost, provided by God, and somehow we were under it and were made to feel like His children and also surrounded by the love of our worldly family.*

Christina is clear that such validation has had a profoundly liberating effect in her life:

> *Following the civil partnership, and the experience of it, the sense of validation was greater, that it was an experience that was of itself a strengthening experience...significantly in the wider context of the recognition of it in the relationship, both internally but also in terms of people's reactions to it, which include the family reactions. And that since then, which is eight years now, that seems to have been a process of deepening and strengthening.*

Living with the threat of violence

The most shocking moments of the research process arose from my realization of the amount of violence, bullying and sexual abuse almost all the participants had known. Two had known sexual abuse as children or young people. Vanessa describes this within the context of bullying in childhood:

> *I was kind of 'outed' when I was at school...and it went horribly wrong. And I shaved my hair and was quite a tomboy. I got, like, severely bullied at school, beaten up, and I didn't go to school for nearly two years... We had to move town because I couldn't go into town because people would, like, beat me up.*
>
> *And then my father was very much against me being gay so that was really hard... Obviously I can't say categorically if I hadn't been abused by my dad then I wouldn't be gay, or I would be gay. All I know is what's true to me, which is that I'm gay.*

For Vanessa, awareness that she is gay became inextricably linked with the feeling of being deserving of punishment. The guilt involved in being abused became attached to being guilty for being gay.

Ted had known sexual abuse as a child and had been beaten up in the street as an adult, while Stephen, like Vanessa, had known violent bullying when younger:

> *Beaten up, trying to remember... I was cornered and threatened with violence. At school I was bullied very heavily. I was bullied when I was a young child by other children. I was bullied again as a teenager by the sort of popular guy at school when his mates decided to corner me*

> *at the back of the corridor and threatened to tell my father that I was a*
> *poofter. I had people calling me names, doing kind of mincing sounds.*

For other participants, violence remains a threat. For three female participants, this threat appears to be linked with outward appearance, being lesbian and pregnant, or being lesbian and appearing masculine. Emma ponders this risk further in these terms:

> *I get looked up and down in a hostile way, by men particularly. Because*
> *of that 'What are you – man, woman? I can't place you.' I am not*
> *obviously female enough. I am a woman and I feel perfectly happy in*
> *my female body and wouldn't want to alter it at all. But other people*
> *can react with hostility to that not quite knowing…*

For one participant, this not quite knowing what will happen next, in terms of threatened hostility towards her partner, is very stressful:

> *It also affects things like when we are going away on holiday or at*
> *weekends, we are always very conscious of who's going to book into the*
> *hotel, how is it going to look, is this going to be a problem? It doesn't*
> *matter that it's illegal here for people not to admit us, it's just that we*
> *don't want to deal with that hassle. Um, yes, so I would say it has caused*
> *significant difficulties. Mostly, I would say it's about always being wary*
> *of being put on the spot, what people are going to do, what's going to*
> *happen next? And that creates a bit of stress, not between us, but it*
> *means that we cannot relax in the same way that other couples do.*

Only half joking, one female participant describes the challenge of remaining safe:

> *I suppose there is a little bit of me that thinks it's the lesser of two evils*
> *that they think I am a man, as opposed to a butch lesbian, because*
> *then I may not get my head kicked in.*

Three research participants have known bullying in the context of work. Anne describes the fear caused by this for her, and the effort to remain brave on behalf of others:

> *I have seen that [bullying] happening with other people, in terms of the comments made about people who are gay, or perceived as gay, particularly gay men rather than lesbians. I always challenge those comments but thinking nervously, this is about to turn on me. Yes, it does go as far as bullying.*

While civil partnership cannot act as a panacea to solve the problem of the violence and bullying caused by homophobic hate, it nonetheless offers liberation in two distinct ways. First, it reflects and consolidates a sense of greater tolerance towards gay and lesbian people in society, and as such is to be supported, as David suggests:

> *I see it also as important to me in my place in society, for all sorts of reasons, but it's partly about a form of equal recognition. It's not the same as marriage quite but it felt like that. And it's partly too, to address some of the consequences of the way gay people have been treated unequally for so long.*

Second, it helps also to create a sense, by virtue of the trust involved in declaring a permanent commitment, of home as a place of non-threat, of haven, of alternative non-competitive values. Anne describes the importance of creating a 'no-blame culture', and Emma of enjoying ordinariness, quoting Wendy Cope's (2001) poem 'Being Boring':

> *Someone to stay home with was all my desire*
> *And, now that I've found a safe mooring,*
> *I've just one ambition in life: I aspire*
> *To go on and on being boring.*

A spiritual wilderness

A sharp sense of alienation is also described by nine participants in terms of their relationship with God at certain points in their lives. They speak of wrestling with God, as Jacob with the angel, in the quest to gain a greater sense of self-assurance and confidence. Sue gives an example of a conversation running with God earlier in her life, first about her own identity, then about her lesbian partnership:

> *I struggled in the early days about when I first realized that I was a lesbian, I mean way back then, with the whole God/lesbian thing... At first I couldn't see how on earth these two things could be remotely compatible. I worked that through over a period of time. So now I suppose that I am in a position where I think that something so good and something so pure – pure is not quite the right word, but sort of, good and honest and truthful and faithful – can't be wrong but must have something 'God-ish' about it...*

Her working it through involved thinking and praying to God as Creator:

> *There was a one-way conversation and I said, 'It follows that you must have made me like this. You have either made a mess of this, which I can't believe, or it's true, this is the situation. So, the only other option is you made me, and I happen to be a lesbian so...' So, I came to be at peace with myself about it I suppose. I couldn't understand how it could be all right, but surely it must be because, you know, there were parameters – not sleeping around, not being destructive, the same as if I had been heterosexual – so in the context of a stable, loving, monogamous relationship it must be all right. So, I sort of came to peace with it.*

She describes how her relationship enables her to be more Christ-like:

> *'God-ish'... Or perhaps better Christ-like. It sounds a bit pretentious but you know a snapshot of the Divine, you know that whole thing about honesty and truth and openness and kindness and love, you know things in Corinthians about what love is, they are all pictures of God, aren't they? So I suppose in that sense – I don't think of it as holy exactly, but then I don't think of any relationship as holy, but it does have elements of, good elements in it, which are from God.*

For Lucy, there was a struggle to understand how she could be Christian and lesbian and a mother:

> *In the past I found myself battling against myself, and my faith helped me to go easy on myself, and to forgive myself. Not that I think that*

> *I needed forgiving, but I tried so hard NOT to be gay and…yes…but, because I really, really wanted children, that's what I wanted more, really. I couldn't work that out… I thought I would have a headache for the rest of my life. I had to get through that to go, 'This is pointless, why am I doing this to myself?'*

Finding a partner plays an important part in healing the relationship with God. As many as nine interviewees describe the importance of finding a partner with faith. Anne's partner brought her back to church and to a deeper sense of faith in God. For Stephen and David, such a shared Christian faith was essential to the bonding of the relationship:

> *Love, mutual respect, self-sacrifice, and also hope. Um, commitment, dedication, and you know I think that that all is derived from [our Christian faith], and I take great comfort from the fact that all these are reciprocated I think, because largely we are, we have a Christian belief system. We believe in Christ and I think that I don't have a reason to doubt any of these things because that's what fundamentally he believes.*

Lillian expresses the urgency for her of finding a partner sympathetic to her Christian faith very early in her life, despite that being difficult:

> *I remember having some quite bruising lesbian relationships with women who were very hostile to Christianity, and saying, 'I am a Christian and I go to church and if that's going to be a problem, this isn't going to work out.'*

For Emma, falling in love with her partner and falling in love with God happened at the same time:

> *I was not exactly an atheist when I met my partner, but I was certainly not at all churched, not interested in church at all. I started going to church because it was important to her. And then it became important to me, by stealth [laughs]. Falling in love with my partner was a bit like falling in love with God.*

Christina describes in clear terms how her knowledge of God has been affected and deepened for her by entry into civil partnership:

> *I think I am fundamentally altered by this whole experience, so that my faith and values and worldview are not the same. So yes. I think it leads me to be profoundly grateful and my faith is changed by that. That instead of having a sense of incompleteness and craving in life, where my faith would be partly trying to resolve those questions, this gives me a much, I suppose really such a profound sense of love that my understanding of the love of God is deeply influenced by it.*

What I find striking is that neither the quest for God nor the quest for love was sacrificed or ignored by the interviewees. The experience of love, the safety, challenge, forgiveness and creativity that love brings to these research participants, persuades them that this queer love is of God.

Is this liberation theology?

Do these accounts amount to a collective theology of liberation? There was one interviewee who stood out as having definitely developed his own gay liberation theology, namely Ted. Ted is a lay theologian, who as a student at an American university was influenced by pastoral chaplains steeped in an understanding of liberation theology. They applied this theology to help students accept and enjoy their bodies and their emerging sexual identity, whether this identity was gay or straight. Ted knew Robert Goss, who wrote *Jesus Acted Up: A Gay and Lesbian Manifesto* (1993) and was particularly encouraged by the idea that gay couples may be fruitful in terms of their community action in much the same way that the lives of members of a religious community may be 'fruitful'. Ted now chooses to worship in communities that identify with people who live on the margins of society, and when he gets married will do so at Dignity, New York, his church community when he is in the United States:

> *The New York thing we anticipate will be the sacrament of marriage,*
> *even though it's officially illicit, from the Roman Catholic hierarchical*
> *point of view. But that's what makes it so nice!*

But Ted's account aside, I was still left with the question of whether it is possible, or indeed helpful, to consider the remaining stories from the rest of my interviewees as theologies of liberation, especially where research participants make no explicit reference to it. What is liberation theology, and is the sort of knowledge it reveals demonstrated in these narratives?

The development of queer liberation theology

In 1971, Gustavo Guttiérez, then professor at the Pontifical Catholic University of Peru, published his seminal work, *A Theology of Liberation*. This was the fruit of the reflection by Latin American theologians in the 1960s that a Christian interpretation of history was needed that was linked to social engagement and action. In Latin America by the end of the 1960s, it was mostly articulated by reference to Marxist analysis, which demonstrated how economic development for some parts of society was linked with underdevelopment for others. Waves of populist movements had previously struggled to address the poor socio-economic conditions of the rural peasants and shanty-town dwellers, whose lot was not improved by the rise of industrial development, which brought wealth only to the middle and urban working classes. Finding support for an emphasis on human advancement and social progress emerging from many of the official Roman Catholic Church documents of the Second Vatican Council, many Latin American theologians, among others, sought to develop a theology from the impoverished margins of society, which focused primarily on the concerns of those people living on the extreme margins of absolute poverty. A contemporary British liberation theologian, Christopher Rowland, underlines the potent catechetical and missional power of doing theology in this way:

> God's Word is to be found in the dialectic between the literary memory of the people of God and the continuing story to be

discovered in the contemporary world, particularly among those people with whom God has chosen to be identified. (2007, p.8)

Yet, as Liberation Theology matured and developed it received sustained critique from many factions within and external to the Church. There are two forms of this critique that are significant for this research, and that I will now focus on. Marcella Althaus-Reid, a Latin American theologian, while grateful to her forebears in liberation theology, nonetheless accused those same theologians of galvanizing the prevailing if often invisible ideologies of race, gender and sexuality inherent in their work. Althaus-Reid observed that the lived, embodied reality of the poor is that they are people of different ethnic, sexual and gender identities (2007, p.126). Those identities determine how even poverty itself may be structured around the binaries of male/female; normal/abnormal; orthodox/heterodox; saint/sinner, and so on.

Althaus-Reid contended that this type of hierarchical thinking, with its undergirding structures of power, needs to be submitted to the challenge of queer theology in order to begin to deconstruct the theological discourse of a Church intent, Althaus-Reid believed, on controlling human sexuality. 'It is time', she wrote, 'to liberate people, and also God, from the oppression of centuries of injustice and abuse towards those who do not partake of patriarchal, heterosexual ideologies' (p.128). This is to be done by doing what Althaus-Reid calls 'honest theology', which is, she suggests, 'a theology able to reflect on the lives of the people and the manifestations of God in our communities, beyond the dogma of a sexual ideology such as heterosexuality' (p.134). Althaus-Reid believed that one way of doing such honest theology was for gay and lesbian people to tell their stories to and for the Church: 'The powerful theological praxis of transformation usually comes from the direction of aliens working within the system' (2000, p.30). This research process created the context for gay and lesbian people to do that: to tell their stories of committed faithful love to and for the Church.

The question arises at this point of how story turns into theology. Is queer liberation theology simply a matter of telling the stories of gay and lesbian lives in the context of the Church? What sort of theological knowledge is gained from the analysis of these stories? When I identify research participants' experiences of God in the everyday life of their relationships, is it possible to combine their language of lived human experience with descriptions of the divine and infinite?

In 'Action Is the Life of All', the practical theologian Zoë Bennett (2007, p.41) asks the same sort of question – namely, what sort of knowledge will such an analysis deliver? Bennett's suggestion is that human story becomes Christian theology where the language of that story reflects the teller's engagement with themes of the Christian tradition. If the stories of these research participants constitute fragments of theology, we may find in them signs of active participation in the process of integrating Christian faith with life, coupled with a recognition that whatever knowledge of God we possess it is provisional knowledge, since we cannot fully penetrate the mystery of God. We will find signs of belief in Jesus as the Son of God, and in the Holy Spirit as agent of liberation. We may expect to find an awareness of the doctrine of creation, of the longing to gather with other Christians as church community, and of the need for giving away the knowledge of the love and justice of God in mission (Bennett 2007, pp.49–51).

In summary, in returning to the narratives of my research participants, if I seek in these accounts a Christian theology of queer liberation, it must also reflect my awareness of these two basic critiques. Queer liberation theology reflects an emancipatory awareness that sexuality is ideologically constructed, while remaining firmly rooted in the struggle to create a transcendent Christian theology that does justice to diverse human experiences and in which there is attention given to the presence and voice of God known in Christ, through the Holy Spirit, and in the community of faith.

A queer liberation theology of civil partnership
Theology that is participative and provisional

Research participants all engaged in a creative discussion about the theological meaning of civil partnership. They were open to new meanings revealed to them in the process of this discussion. Sue was caused to think about whether God works in human history. Lucy reflected how the experience of her relationship revealed aspects of God as patience, forgiveness and tolerance. Lillian found that the discussion liberated her into a new way of understanding her relationship as prophetic of God's future. Participants sensed their understandings to be provisional as they explored the meaning of God for their lives, and also grappled with the status of their relationships given that same-sex civil marriage was on the horizon of possibility for them.

However, they had already participated in creating theology and had themselves liberated language about God from silence and secrecy. It is not only the participants who were led from wilderness to homecoming by their engagement in civil partnership, but language about God was liberated also. Despite the legal injunction not to mention God in the civil ceremony, seven participants found ways of expressing their faith there, for example by using silence and candlelight, or by finding poems, music and song that spoke to them of God. Anne was delighted that by using the song 'Something Inside So Strong' by Labi Siffre she was able to give a religious flavour to her civil partnership rite. The lyrics of this popular song describe the walls of the city of Jericho falling before an incoming army, as lies are demolished by truth telling. The story from the Old Testament book of Joshua describing the new and blessed life of the people of God is there, albeit hidden in a secular song.

The presence of God was also acknowledged by Anne and her partner in the song 'I'll Walk Beside You',[1] which she and her partner interpreted as God's promise to walk beside them. Ted re-wrote the biblical story of Ruth and Naomi[2] as a poem, omitted the word *God*, and was permitted by the registrar to use the poem as the basis of his civil partnership vows. Christina found a song that had become a famous song of lament for justice in the Quaker movement. Sue wrote to the *Church Times* that God was of course present at the rite since God is everywhere, and is in all things, even if the couple were forced to exchange their vows silently before Him. Lillian used silence

---

1   'I'll Walk Beside You' is a 1939 love song written by Alan Murray and Edward Lockton. The singer John McCormack made it particularly famous.

2   Ruth 1:8–22.

and candlelight, with readings from Alice Walker's novel *The Color Purple* and from the speeches of Martin Luther King to express the couple's spirituality:

> *We couldn't have religious readings, but we tried to make them religious. And the registrar was going to pass as much as he could without getting into trouble. He was very nice, kind of priestly.*

Hearing how insistently interviewees found ways to give theological content to these civil public rites I began to name them 'Coming Out Ceremonies for God', places where the queer God was named in non-sacred texts and was heard to speak even in silence.

In addition to the civil rite celebrated in register offices, nine participants also held religious celebrations of their partnership in Church. The size and shape of these celebrations varied widely. Christina and her partner held a tiny ceremony of silence with four friends before the larger civil partnership celebration. Robert and Tom held a large event which Tom does not describe as religious but honouring the different spirituality of many people:

> *We took account of the spirit of humanity, celebration and love, and wove these through song, readings, talk and laughter into the fabric of the service that we ourselves put together.*

Three other couples held services of thanksgiving and dedication in the context of the Eucharist, in very different styles of service. For two couples, these were understood to be for them services of 'marriage', while the third couple anticipate a future service of marriage in the United States. What all three couples acknowledge is an awareness of the presence of God and God's blessing for them. Matthew recalls how 'the Christian magic happened' when in the raising of the bread and wine he saw himself and his partner raised, held, blessed and sent out to witness to their faith in the world. Stephen was overwhelmed by an awareness of the love of God. Lillian recalls the sense of sacramental presence filling the church and the rite for her:

> *All I know is that when we had the first ceremony that was a spiritual experience. We were attending Christians, in a church community, we arrived at the church and the nuns were dotted around the church, you know, they were there praying. And for me I had no idea they were going to do that. They were invited as guests, but for me as soon as I arrived that was a physical outward sign that I'm going, this is a sacrament, like getting ordained. This part is a spiritual sacrament.*

This inclusion of God where 'God' has been officially silenced is particularly meaningful given a context in which the language of the quadruple lock has been used to safeguard the Church of England from being forced to perform rites of same-sex marriage. God cannot be locked out from the celebratory marking of these relationships, since God is present and active in the participants, who are Church, ecclesia, gatherings of Christians to worship. The research participants, under the threat of exclusion and experiencing the mystery of God's being even in that exclusion, created liturgy, of which the Brazilian philosopher and Episcopalian priest Maraschin exclaims: 'It is liturgy. It is the action of the people gathered for experiencing and experimenting with the joy of being alive. It is bewilderment in the face of the abyss and under the threat of nothing' (2009, p.176). This awareness of an active liberating God is, again, cause for the Church to rejoice.

Theology that is Christological

Participants all spoke of knowing Christ in two specific ways in relation to the experience of civil partnership, namely as inspiration of God, and as presence of God.

Jesus meets Anne in the wilderness of her fear and supports her where her own courage fails:

> *I very much believe in, um, the life of Jesus and the way he behaved, in terms of recognizing people on the margins. That gives me the strength to think, well actually, whatever happens in terms of announcements about what's going to happen in the Church of England, which upset us on a regular basis...whatever happens in that, I really do firmly believe that if Jesus was here, he would say what a good relationship you two*

> *have got, and encourage it, and that does strengthen me. Because there*
> *are times when it seems like nobody is on side...*

Christina is inspired by Christ seeing beneath the surface of our scapegoating vulnerable others:

> *Jesus's careful and effective challenging of those assumptions of the*
> *religious authority, and replacing that with an expression of love,*
> *containment, protection.*

Other participants find in their loving relationship a manifestation of Christ's love. Many, like Sue, emphasize a newness of life lived in forgiveness:

> *This is the first relationship I have ever had – I have had three – it's the*
> *longest and most adult of course, but also it's the relationship in which*
> *I don't have any fear about doing things wrong. That's not to say that*
> *I don't do anything wrong, I mess up. But I think we bring out the best*
> *in each other so I don't feel so fearful and I don't get things wrong so*
> *much and it's a kind of cyclical thing.*

Vanessa finds Christ looking at her out of her partner's face, and particularly in the way each makes sacrifices for the other:

> *I do see Christ in Alice every day, which makes me smile, or even*
> *when we have an argument. I mean, we have both sacrificed a lot for*
> *each other.*

Stephen too finds reminders of Christ's sacrifice in his hopes for his relationship:

> *So, the idea of self-sacrifice for the other, which is helpful in marriage,*
> *I can see is clearly derived from the idea of Christ's sacrifice in the*
> *Christian tradition. It permeates our thinking throughout our existence,*
> *hopefully. So in this relationship where you hold the deepest love, which*
> *you are so engaged in, you would put that into action even more,*
> *because of the proximity and relevance of it.*

Sue knows Christ in terms of hoping to become more Christ-like in relationship:

> I am probably at my best when I am loved, obviously, I mean we all are. So, I am more like Christ although still a long way off.

In summary, participants revealed a mature and deep awareness of Christ, fully human and fully God, in their relationships, and of how they know him, primarily as liberator making present God's sacrifice, forgiveness and love.

Theology of the spirit

Matthew and Vanessa give the fullest descriptions of understanding the role of the Holy Spirit in their lives. Vanessa understands the Spirit to blossom in power when she and her partner spend time together:

> It's like an energy that burns inside but is free as well. And that Spirit is sometimes released when Alice and me are together sometimes. The Spirit is let out rather than being contained in.

Matthew lives under the guidance and promptings of the Holy Spirit, who continually puts people and tasks into Matthew's way:

> The Holy Spirit puts different things into my lap to do.

He enjoyed a vision of the church celebration of his relationship as an event in which he and his partner were lifted, supported and sent out like Jesus in his baptism. From that point he believed the Spirit changed his understanding of his relationship. It had now, he was surprised to discover, become a channel to be used by God and directed by God's Spirit:

> I think we keep thinking, what is the relationship between us and the rest of society? I have sensitivity towards what the Holy Spirit wants me to do next. The radar is full on.

There are signs of profound connection made between the life of the relationship and the divine life. Four couples pray together, as Stephen describes here:

> That sense of kneeling and seeking, praying. That is definitely something which we experience as a pattern in our relationship. The sort of seeking guidance, seeking peace, seeking hope again, um, praying together, that is a very important building block of our relationship.

Lucy sits studying the Bible at home in the company of her partner and child, seeking a faith that concerns the whole of life:

> I'll sit here with my Bible study books and that's just how we are. It needs to be part of your whole life rather than just when I am at church.

Robert describes this awareness of God's presence simply, perhaps with an unconscious reference to the brooding of the Spirit:

> It's the relationship that matters, and this is like a rare and very beautiful bird.

Yet the Holy Spirit is mentioned less consistently than the other two Persons of the Trinity. It is possible that Emma, in relation to seeing a picture of ecstatic worship or praise, stumbles across a reason for this. Emma enjoys throwing herself deeply into experiences. She is attracted to the worship style of charismatic praise and prayer. Yet she believes that she cannot risk the disapproval she fears may accompany more conservative expressions of faith. It is possible that language rich with resonances about the Holy Spirit has become largely the possession of the charismatic evangelical church:

> I have always been drawn to ecstatic worship. But I can't go there because of what that's bundled with. But if fundamentalist Christians weren't so fucking horrible about us, I would be a fundamentalist, it's my personality. I would give it 100 per cent, you know, that giving everything, because I like to dive in, I like to be immersed in experience.

The doctrine of creation

How do the research participants understand themselves within creation? Do they hold essentialist beliefs about their sexuality, understanding that they were born gay and lesbian, bisexual or gender queer, and created such by God? Or do they understand themselves to have constructed their identity from a complex web of choices and opportunities open to them? How do they understand the determination of their sexuality in a theological sense?

Seven participants appear to hold an essentialist view, that sexual orientation is an objective, transcultural fact, and that they themselves have a stable sexual identity which is lesbian or gay. Four others, a second group, have attempted to live other sexual identities, either as part of sexual exploration as they grew into adulthood, or, for one, because it was culturally dangerous to be 'out'. All four demonstrate a sense of liberation in finding and establishing themselves in their present identity. Only two, a third group, are queer in a constructivist sense, experiencing themselves and others to have a fluid gender and sexual identity. One challenges the fixed binary identities of lesbian and gay and calls herself 'gay-ish'. The other is aware of possessing what others understand to be distinctly masculine and feminine features and, similarly eschewing the labels lesbian and gay, describes herself as genderqueer.

What are the implications of these understandings for this research? I discovered that the first group believe themselves to have been created gay and lesbian by God. This belief provides the grounds for self-belief and growth in self-confidence. David explains:

> We are all created in the image of God. And essentially because I know what is good within me, and what is not, I have never had a moral or a religious problem with my sexuality. That goes back to my creation as a child of God in the image of God as we all are.

When she was younger, essentialist belief undergirded the conversations in which Sue reasoned with God about her own future:

> There was a one-way conversation and I said, 'It follows that you must have made me like this. You have either made a mess of this, which I

> can't believe, or it's true, this is the situation. So, the only other option
> is you made me, and I happen to be a lesbian so...'

The second group is intriguing, perhaps because it represents most closely my own journey. For them liberation was experienced not from continuing to adopt and experiment with different and opposite sexual identities but from choosing to be known to both self and others as gay or lesbian, even at the expense of battling with inner fears and outer disapproval. Lucy describes the relief involved in allowing herself to be lesbian:

> ...the last two relationships I had been in had been really manky, really,
> and just hard work. So, it was, to me, like, 'This is who I am, and this
> is what I want.'

For Matthew the prize for the struggle is the freedom to be his authentic self-in-relationship:

> I think it's about five years, between the start of the healing process and
> the civil partnership.

God is evident for Matthew in this process, as he becomes less self-obsessed with trying to conform to heteronormative patterns of living, and more able to be transformed in the direction of self-giving towards his partner.

The two who declared a constructivist view by challenging the title 'lesbian' at the beginning of their interviews stand out among this group of research participants for celebrating a same-sex wedding in church many years before their rite of civil partnership, and therefore finding the registration of civil partnership slightly less significant for them. They are more critical of the heteropatriarchy of the Church of England than are other research participants, and more restless in their attitude towards settling in any one Anglican congregation or alternative church. The diversity of God's queer creation was expressed in a party following their wedding, at which it proved impossible to have 'straight' dance columns:

> *In the evening we had a ceilidh and the whole parish came. There was a caller from church and there was a laugh with that because he said, 'If we could have, if we could have ladies on the left and men on the left,' and sort of...and all the gay people said... 'Oh, all right then, we'll have some of you on the left and some of you on the right' [laughter]. And we had, you know, lesbians and nuns dancing!*

At this point it becomes obvious that I am using the words *queer* and *queer theology* in a loose rather than a narrow sense. I reject fundamentalism in relation to queer and queer theology. I acknowledge that detectable in these narratives are strands of orthodox belief, of gay and lesbian protest theology, of essentialist and constructivist views about human sexuality, and of queer liberation theology. I claim the word *queer* for these theologies believing that they reflect something of what Althaus-Reid called 'manifestations of God in our communities, beyond the dogma of a sexual ideology such as heterosexuality' (2007, p.134). Here are queer people using theology to interrogate patterns of heteronormative belief, liturgy and life. Here are her 'aliens within the system', questioning it from the inside.

Belonging as church

A striking distinction is made by almost all research participants between the enjoyment of being part of the congregation of a parish church, in this case St Martin-in-the-Fields, and the disappointment and hurt caused by formal Church statements voicing disapproval of gay and lesbian people and of their committed long-term relationships. All the female research participants – Emma, Lillian, Sue, Anne, Christina, Lucy and Vanessa – have in their past spent time, whether months or years, away from church belonging, rather than continuing to experience this hurt. Four participants experienced rejection or hurt from family members on religious grounds. Many more experienced the disapproval of church members where they formerly belonged. All 13 participants experienced as deeply painful the negativity expressed over long-term gay and lesbian relationships in official statements of the Church of England.

Two participants have rejected the Church of England as a place for them to grow spiritually. Emma has left, yet mourns the community she once enjoyed, stating:

> The rising tide of homophobia has put paid to, at least for the present time, my desire to express my faith through Church.

Her faith in God living at the heart of her partnership, however, remains strong:

> ...when we married in 1995, we viewed the marriage as a three-way relationship, between us and God...without God this three-legged stool would fall over.

Tom has rejected Christianity and has embarked on a quite other spiritual journey, which for him spells freedom:

> I know nothing of the traditional Christian view of God anywhere, either in marriage or out, in CP or out. 'God' as conceived and perceived in conventional Christianity has no meaning for me. What I know of my spiritual existence, and the great benefit and pleasure I derive from being present, not dwelling in the past, or in a fantasy future, and in shedding the chains of an obsession with sin and an all-demanding, never-satisfied 'God', has nothing at all to do with marriage, CP or any other human-created institution.

Two participants, by contrast, react with patience to hurtful statements, aided by their understanding of the slow progress of institutional change. David suggests:

> Synod has sometimes to me in recent years seemed like a hostile environment, a hostile organization, kind of alien to me. And that's because of the gay issue. I feel it vicariously for women too. But as someone who, as I said earlier, quite likes institutions, I have a double take on that. And I do believe in the institution of the Church and that Synod is part of that. And I think that sometimes one just has to be patient.

Stephen, similarly, reacts negatively to individual Church leaders and Synod members, but does not believe that the Church as an institution is to be hated:

> I am angry with individuals and not with institutions. That's generally in my life the case. I belong to a lot of institutions which are riddled with individuals with whom I can have incredibly long arguments, but I don't want to dismiss an institution on the basis of some offensive individuals. They are groups of people. People personalize institutions and that's unhelpful.

Despite these negative feelings, most research participants live their Christian discipleship in the context of disciplined church attendance and belonging at St Martin's, which was sought out by 11 of the participants for its open inclusion of gay and lesbian people. Ted suggests it was known to him as 'the foremost church open and affirming to gay and lesbian people', while Lucy, coming to live and work in London for the first time, looked it up on gay-friendly websites and was reassured by its emphasis on 'inclusion'.

For five participants church belonging is experienced as spiritually transformative. Vanessa's story bears striking witness to the power of theology and the welcoming community at St Martin's to transform life. She had known violence and abuse in her upbringing and had found no place of acceptance of her lesbian identity in the Catholic Church of her childhood. In addition, she suffered serious illness. Despite this, she was a creative person in a happy civil partnership when seven years ago, seeking to integrate her awareness of God with her sexual orientation as lesbian, she found herself at St Martin-in-the-Fields. She describes the effect of realizing through listening to lectures and sermons, by making friends, and using the building when quiet to meditate, a sense of being utterly loved by God:

> St Martin's was a safe place for me to explore my sexuality and my faith together. Before I hadn't found a place to do that. I had to shut the door on Catholicism for a time before I revisited what I thought of God and what my faith was. It was in St Martin's that I realized, going to the lectures, things like that, you know intellectually stimulating things, it

> *was okay to be gay, and to still be loved by God. And that's something*
> *that I have always struggled with my whole life.*

Vanessa had always worried that her lesbian identity was linked with the violent abuse of her childhood, that it had a thoroughly evil origin and root. She was set free from this fear by attending a lecture, 'Wholly, Holy', given by the Vicar of St Martin-in-the-Fields, the Revd Dr Samuel Wells, which was later published in a series of essays *How Then Shall We Live?* (Wells 2016). By studying this, she was enabled to understand herself and her relationship as a gift of God to Church and world:

> *That's what I took from that lecture. I read it, took my time over it. It's*
> *a gift, not something that I am damaged by!*

At the time of the research interview, Vanessa was a very active member of the community at St Martin's, while the security of living in civil partnership had allowed her a more thorough exploration of faith.

David explains how being fully accepted deepens faith and relationship with God since nothing needs to be hidden at St Martin-in-the-Fields, either in conversation or in prayer:

> *The convenient way of dealing with that in so many churches is to*
> *leave your difficult issues at the door of the church. You don't bring your*
> *sexuality in. You would find yourself able to go to church, communicate*
> *with God on a personal level but then go and have coffee afterwards and*
> *find yourself unwilling to talk about who you were going on holiday with.*

Transformative too is the awareness among the participants that St Martin-in-the-Fields allowed itself to be engaged and changed in the process of attempting to transform others. Those who asked for a service to celebrate their civil partnership, or who asked for their children to be baptized, played a large part in developing the services. Both the church leadership team and members of the congregation absorbed anxiety over possible protest, heard and performed readings and prayers containing pain and celebration, and attended in support, even where this demanded a change of heart over the acceptableness of homosexual relationships. The welcoming community of St Martin's was experienced as stretched, both momentarily in particular liturgical and educational moments, and permanently in terms of the community's shape, to welcome the queer stranger. Matthew describes the vital importance to him of this sense of reciprocal supportive community:

> I think that in the Holy Spirit we were lifted, the symbol is lifted, visible, and supported. So, it's just part of the process that we receive the additional strength of being supported, but that with that strength we have more capacity to, um, think about our position for the community.

Mission and witness

I discovered that research participants set their stories of liberation in a theological context. In the case of all but one, who understands his liberation to have involved stepping outside Christianity, they understand themselves to have been liberated in some sense by God, who is Creator, Jesus Christ and Holy Spirit. Liberated themselves, do they have an attitude of responsibility towards others, to share their experience of liberation? Is there a sense of mission and witness present in their theologies?

For three participants there is a sense of responsibility for bearing witness to their faith in ways sensitive to their partner's needs. One, Anne, comes to church again regularly, and eagerly follows a life of faith as a result of her partner's persuasion that she need not worship the Established Church, but God. The partners of the remaining two attend church activities as supporters and respect their partner's positions as Christians.

All participants suggest that their partnership has involved them in a sense of responsibility for family, for being honest with and caring towards both their own family of origin and the family of their partner. Anne speaks of growing closeness to her partner's family:

> I have developed a very close relationship with her parents. I love them and am very fond of them. That's been really good in terms of

> *supporting them and my partner when her brother died, because they did feel they could talk to me, and do feel they can talk to me.*

She also speaks of the more difficult engagement with her own family members in being clear about her own relationship status even where that takes courage, and of her partner's gentle help in that process.

Six participants take an active and deliberative role in mission as gay and lesbian Christians, though in colourfully different ways. Lucy is able to bear witness to her Christian faith to her neighbours who question her about her regular attendance at church, as does Sue to her work colleagues. For Ted and Matthew, it was important to bear witness by entering the Gay Pride March on the very day of their civil partnership. Stephen and David were glad to come out as both Christian and gay, to family and work colleagues, at the celebration of their civil partnership in church.

Eleven participants seek greater justice for lesbian and gay members of church and society. Christina, Lillian and Emma, Ted and Matthew have actively campaigned for this; Lillian, Emma and Ted all at times changed town and work circumstances to do so. David accepts that the challenge of the Gospel does not end with furthering lesbian and gay rights and is particularly challenged by the existence of world poverty, as Matthew is by ecological issues, Christina and Vanessa by mental health issues. In all participants there is a sense of being freed by security in relationship to care for others, as Emma summarizes:

> *I think I have contributed more to society because I have been happier, it's made me look beyond myself more.*

Conclusion

In the stories of these research participants I find fragments of a queer liberation theology of civil partnership. While the participants have no collective understanding of a shared way forward, the expectation that they adopt a common liberation theology, of identical methods and strategies of struggle, would subvert queer theology's emphasis on the acceptance of difference. They are, however, in clear agreement over three issues. First, they are disappointed over the Church of England's lack of formal statements of support for gay and lesbian people and their relationships. Second, they find rich theological meaning and reasons for faith and hope in God in their rites and relationships of civil partnership. Third, they frequently raise the question of their relationships of civil partnership: 'Is this marriage, or not?' Before answering the question 'Is this marriage, or not?', I notice the that word they don't share as a group to describe their lives and relationships is the word *queer*. Why, then, do I choose to use it? What is the value of queer theology on this journey towards understanding marriage in a new theological light?

Chapter 4

SOMETHING BORROWED, SOMETHING NEW

What Is Queer Theology?

A journey in understanding

As I begin writing this chapter, which concerns an encounter with queer history and theology experienced as birth pangs towards a new understanding of God, I recall these words from a poem by the monastic author and poet Thomas Merton (1985):

> *All theology is a kind of birthday*
> *Each one who is born*
> *Comes into the world as a question*
> *For which old answers*
> *Are not sufficient.*

I grew up in a part of rural England so isolated in the 1950s and 60s that a whiff of Thomas Hardy's Dorset lingered. In that environment the word *queer* meant strange or odd, and only in late adolescence did I register it as a derogatory term used of men suspected of being homosexual. How did the same word become an expression of empowerment, and a descriptor of a type of critical theory and theology? No one is certain, but the development, perhaps beginning in the coalition of people of all sexualities forced into co-operation by the AIDS crisis, was complete by the late 1980s when gay and bisexual activist groups coined the title 'Queer Nation' and their slogan 'We're here! We're queer! Get used to it!'

The challenge of 'queer'

Queer theology borrows language and methodology from queer theory. Queer theory is concerned to explore the ways in which heterosexuality is deemed normative in our society. It asks the question of how homosexuality is constructed in many cultures as abnormal. In early dialogue, some LGBT theologians simply aligned queer with being LGBT. I was influenced by these writers who, like early feminist theologians, discovered 'places to stand' in biblical and liturgical texts (Ruether 1993[1]). I remember reading a Gospel passage re-scripting the woman bent double before Jesus as a lesbian caught in the silence of homophobic intolerance, at a large public service for LGBT Christian protesters gathered to welcome Bishop Gene Robinson to this country in 1996.[2] Tears streamed down my face as I realized the magnitude of what I was doing. Never, in a lifetime of approximately 10,000 church services attended or performed, had the Bible specifically addressed me in public in terms of my sexual orientation. Some of these early queer theologians, like John McNeil and Troy Perry, adopted an essentialist stance to suggest that being born gay they had been created not sinful but whole by God (McNeill 1976; Perry 1972). Other writers focused on embodiment, and the ways LGBT love expresses God's love (e.g. Goss 1993). These writers were working through the years in which I was battling to become a woman priest, to find a suitable place of employment and life in the system, and to discover my lesbian identity. They spoke a language I understood of finding places to stand within orthodoxy.

Yet queer theology developed also along other lines. Some queer

---

1 Finding places for women to stand, in terms of experiencing themselves described and addressed in the texts of the Bible and of Church tradition, is a major theme of Ruether's book.

2 Gene Robinson was the first person self-identified as homosexual to be consecrated Bishop in the Episcopal Church of the USA. He subsequently wrote an autobiographical account of this experience: *In the Eye of the Storm* (2008, Seabury Books).

theologians, following critical theorists like Judith Butler, argued
against the usefulness of concepts like 'being born gay'. Butler had been
influenced by post-structuralist writers like Derrida and Foucault, who
argued that the subjective sense of self is neither stable nor discrete but
constructed by meshes of discourse going on all around us. Finding
support for their work in Butler's theory that gender and sexuality are
both social constructions and 'performed' rather than innate (Butler
1990), later queer theologians questioned why Church and society
endorse certain social constructions of sexuality and not others.
Other writers, like Lisa Diamond, went on to ask whether the nature
of human sexuality is definable at all. Diamond's work *Sexual Fluidity*
(2008) demonstrates the results of research into non-exclusivity in
attractions among women, changes in attraction over the lifecycle,
and the capacity for attraction to be person-centred rather than
gender-centred (p.90). Using the idea of the non-definability of human
sexuality, other queer theologians, such as Althaus-Reid and Isherwood
(2007), have stretched the concept of queer to develop a theology that is
deconstructive of theological orthodoxy. They suggest that orthodoxy
has been used to reinforce oppressive norms of heteronormative
authority. For them a queer God challenges all human boundaries
of 'power-in-possession', all suggestions of fixed categories of human
language and description.

At first, not wanting to be considered an outsider in church or
society, I feared the word *queer*, and sensed queer theology in its
development to be dangerous for me to absorb, since I had spent
many years of my life constructing a liveable and employable social
self. The battle for this integration was titanic in terms of both my
mental health and resources used in psychoanalytic psychotherapy.
The health that I now enjoy began with my making a choice, deciding
upon a known identity, allowing myself to belong to a category of
persons known as lesbian, no matter what that meant in terms of a
protesting stance and lost preferment within the institution of my
employment. I have, if you like, stared an abyss of indecision and a
chaos of lack of definition in the face and turned away from both, in
order to create and sustain bonds of affection and spaces of belonging
for myself. Lack of definition appears, at an instinctive level to me,
to be a dilettante and luxurious choice open to those not yet in their

life forced to lose by choosing an unacceptable identity. In this sense I found myself the target of this lament of Althaus-Reid:

> The historical feminist liberationists…have not yet completely come to terms with gender issues beyond the equality paradigm. For them sexuality tends to be seen as a frivolous distraction from issues of social justice and women's rights in the Church. In a sense they see queer theologies as a luxury which only privileged women in academia can afford to pursue. (2008, p.106)

For lesbian and gay Christians, the struggle to speak and to be heard, to stand up and own our identity without fear of disapproval or ridicule, remains an urgent challenge on behalf of all those for whom remaining hidden may involve social exclusion, self-abasement and physical abuse. Nevertheless, I digested Althaus-Reid's 'not yet' and found myself struggling with those words in such a way as to become more open to the usefulness of queer theology for this research when in the summer of 2013 I wandered around an exhibition of the work of the artist R.B. Kitaj, at the Pallant House Gallery in Chichester. Here I found images that spoke more deeply to me of the useful vitality of 'being queer' and 'talking queer' than anything I had yet found in the pages of queer theology.

Comprehending 'queer'

I was immediately fascinated by two aspects of the work of Kitaj. I noticed that he used collage, pieces of photography and film, even texts from politics and poetry, to embed his central figures in their wider literary and political context. As the central figures, unlike in some other collage art, remained clearly and compassionately delineated in bold, beautiful colours, I saw a helpful likeness to what I might try to do in qualitative research: use human narratives and interactive research methods to focus on very particular stories. Research participants would have their own density of unique colour but exist within and against a web of interacting sources of inspiration, situations of personal and political conflict, and spread of ideological and theological concepts, which help create their meaning.

Even more forcefully, Kitaj was obsessed with the theme of the outsider. He was born in the early 20th century in Cleveland, Ohio, the son of a Hungarian father and an American-born Russian-Jewish mother who later married Dr Walter Kitaj, a Viennese Jew. Later, as a painter, he was rejected in England for being too American and in America for spending too long in England. Perhaps seeking a culture other than his own in which to belong more deeply, he lived for considerable lengths of time in Catalonia. That area and people, whose own identity of political and cultural struggle he engaged with seriously, seemed to release in him the possibility of investigating in far greater depth his own Jewish heritage, the 'Jewish Question' and Jewish Kabbala. As if from the inside, he painted the grief of the 20th century, the Holocaust, the Spanish Civil War, the conflicts generated by Marxism, the fate of exploited and mistreated people. Among such people were prostitutes and homosexual men.

Three paintings in the exhibition stood out. In 'If Not, Not' (Livingstone 2010, plate 98), Kitaj makes a study of alienation and decay, depicting the gatehouse at Auschwitz and the devastated landscape in front of it. In 'The Neo-Cubist', his self-portrait as a woman (plate 167), he refers specifically to the public humiliation of gentile women in Nazi Germany who had taken Jewish lovers. In this picture he places his own head on a woman's body and owns her fate. In 'Smyrna Greek (Nikos)', he paints the homosexual poet Cavafy at the door of a brothel where a prostitute wears a diaphanous skirt revealing her sexual organs. Behind her, on the stairs, the figure of Kitaj himself descends the steps of the brothel towards us (plate 128).

Perhaps because Kitaj paints with such compassion and respect for individuals whose searching intelligence shines through, I was reminded forcefully of one of the motivations for my work as a writer and priest. I began in part to understand the gay and lesbian community of Soho, where I had previously been Rector for nine years. At St Martin-in-the-Fields, I was cocooned by the tolerance of middle-class metropolitan London, and by the inclusive atmosphere of a well-heeled liberal Christian congregation, into the forgetfulness of violence towards the outsider. In Soho, I had experienced daily the plight of prostitutes and of brothel users. The murder of neither was unknown in the neighbourhood. I had witnessed the pain and death resulting from a homophobic nail bomb attack. I had seen the hatred against the Church written afterwards, on our church entrance noticeboard. I had led memorial service after memorial service for the gay victims of violence and HIV-related illnesses. Understanding meaning in lesbian and gay relationships requires considering that past too. It is part of what I bring as a writer and priest.

Suddenly, both the violence and the compassionate inclusion of all human beings in Kitaj's work demanded that I look again at queer theology and its implications for this journey. For queer theology demands that we ask ourselves the question of whether we have become inured against the possible pain of concentration on 'outsider-ness' and on the pressures which heteronormativity creates for gay and lesbian people. Perhaps entering civil partnerships and same-sex marriage may represent an easing of this pressure, by conforming to heterosexual norms, queer theorists might suggest. Perhaps by entering civil partnerships or marriage we outsiders may be turning insider, so that we in our turn oppress people who for multiple reasons cannot or will not be so committed? From understanding the painful vantage point of queer outsider-ness, we may ask questions like these. Queer theology provides a tool to interrogate heteronormative understandings of God and of human relationships, both to enrich those understandings, and to subvert them by asking: whom do they exclude? Why they are excluded? And what are the effects of that exclusion?

Directions in queer theology

I wish to examine the positive features of queer theology for this 'journey in understanding', not least for the sake of remembering my own outsider past and that of all LGBTQ people. I do that by examining the work of Elizabeth Stuart and Marcella Althaus-Reid, as well as considering the contributions of other queer theologians.

In *Gay and Lesbian Theologies: Repetitions with Critical Difference* (2003), Stuart begins her support for the development of queer theology from the useful starting point of the Lambeth Conference 1998. At this worldwide conference of Anglican bishops a resolution was adopted that included a strong condemnation of homosexual relationships. The resolution, adopted by a vote of 526 to 70, with 45 abstentions, upheld the biblical understanding of marriage as that between a man and a woman, while rejecting sexual activity by gay men and lesbian women as incompatible with the teaching of Scripture. It opposed the ordination to the priesthood of non-celibate gay men and lesbians, and all recognition or blessing of same-sex unions. Emma, a research participant, like other gay and lesbian Christians in the United Kingdom, concluded that a period of apparently increased tolerance to homosexuality in the Church of England was over:

> That was the first sort of earthquake, you know. I had been okay. I was in a lovely community. I had my wife, I had my love, you know, and everything...everything was happy and then suddenly there was this sort of storm? But it still felt at that point as it if was still sort of theoretical really. It was, well you know that's only the bishops talking amongst themselves and it doesn't really affect me...then I remember we went to Green Belt [an annual arts, faith and justice festival] in about 2000 and Peter Selby (the then Bishop of Worcester) saying, 'Don't make this the issue that determines your faith.' And I cried, and left, because I knew then that it would.

For Stuart, the failure of Western bishops to stand against and dialogue with the homophobia contained in the statements of conservative churches made at this conference demonstrated the lack of potency in liberal gay theologies, and in gay and lesbian liberation theologies, to persuade Christians of the justice of the gay cause. For her, these theologies that place sexuality at the centre of human identity are missing the point. They fail to create a rich theology that disturbs our image of ourselves in the light of God's existence. Always at odds with conservative views of human sexuality that are similarly fixed, they perpetuate an ongoing violent battle within the Church. Queer theology pulls the rug out from under this tiring, unremitting war by questioning the notion of gender and sexual identity:

Sexual and gender identities have to be subverted because they are constructed in the context of power and are part of a matrix of dominance and exclusion. They grate against the sign of baptism. (p.108)

Here Stuart hints at how they are to be subverted. All our cultural identities are placed under 'eschatological erasure' (p.107) in the new belonging of being Church, particularly in the rites of baptism and Eucharist. She argues that by baptism human beings receive an identity that is sheer gift, not a matter of either negotiation or performance. Baptism fills us with a desire for the endlessness that belongs to God alone and erases past longings of desire for other categories of being human that protect and exclude. Here Stephen, a research participant, recalls this sense of the endlessness of God experienced at a service of prayer held following the registration of his civil partnership:

> So it was almost like the social and the spiritual world coming together in this one moment and, and the predominant feeling I would say, the sense that you got by marrying the religious and the social was this absolute explosion of feeling of love, really. I really felt surrounded by love! I mean that not in a two-dimensional way but in a kind of almost three-dimensional way like some sort of umbrella of, a shield almost, provided by God, and somehow we were under it and were made to feel like His children and also surrounded by the love of our worldly people.

Stuart believes Christians are called to live out their culturally negotiated identities in precisely such a way as to expose their non-ultimacy, to take them up into the process of redemption: 'In the Eucharist the Church stands on the edge of heaven and standing on the edge of heaven gender differences dissolve' (2003, p.112). At the Eucharistic service of prayer and thanksgiving following Stephen's civil partnership, he stood in this place. In the readings he had chosen in addition to the biblical readings, the dissolution of gender difference was captured in words from Plato's *Symposium*, where Aristophanes tells a tale of finding one's other half: a tale that includes the appearance of a third gender, the 'androgynous'.

It is important to understand how Stuart uses queer critique to both subvert and enlarge our theological vision of what it is to be human. For Stuart both monastic celibacy and same-sex marriage are necessary for the holiness of the Church, to remind it that gender is not of ultimate concern and that desire has an end beyond human relationships. The Church needs to recover its own queer tradition in order to resolve the crisis it is in over homosexuality and because it needs to restore a sense of what it means for the divine purpose to be fulfilled in us in the here and now of everyday life.

Stuart identifies her work with that of other queer theologians who understand lesbian and gay identities to lack ultimate importance. These identities are cultural phenomena, practised and configured differently in diverse cultural contexts. Michael Vasey (1995), for whom the shape of grace is discovered in the embrace of the outsider, believes gay and lesbian people may have a role to play in reminding and recalling the Church to the vitality of friendship. Lucy, a young research participant, reminds us of the vital nature of this calling for her:

> *Just because carrying on a faith is hard work and I needed the support... coming to London and not knowing anyone, I felt that I should be safe in all respects if I made friends through church and went out with those friends.*

Kathy Rudy (1997), lamenting that gay and lesbian people have become such good mimics of heterosexual families, urges the Church to consider other forms of community life, in which baptism is the common identifier. Lucy acknowledges that the baptism of her children mattered so much that she and her partner were willing to risk staring eyes and disapproving comments. When looking at a picture of St Anne with the Virgin Mary, she laughs over the unorthodox nature of her own creation of family:

> *The only thing about that picture is that if it were my partner there, she would be looking at the baby not me! We would both be looking at the baby! The way my partner and I live is not what I imagine a relationship to be like. We are quite independent in ourselves, but we are still a family unit.*

Eugene Rogers (1999), like Stuart, puts ecclesial identity first. We are all, he considers, in the place of Gentiles whom God has grafted onto the vine of his people by grace. Being first the child of God is important, too, to James Alison (2001), who questions the formation of a gay identity based on resentment and anger. David, a research participant, believes similarly that it is our creation as children of God and our enjoyment of that privilege that constitute our most significant identity:

> We are all created in the image of God. And essentially because I know what is good within me, and what is not, I have never had a moral or a religious problem with my sexuality. That goes back to my creation as a child of God in the image of God as we all are.

Ironically, this deeper identity as children of God may be extremely hard to communicate to others, who may view Christianity and the Church as homophobic in attitude. Here Stephen views his service of prayer and dedication as a sort of 'coming out' as Christian, in the way he describes the difference between the civil rite of civil partnership registration and the later service in church:

> One is the spiritual and religious difference, the fact that the whole day, not just the service itself, the whole day was dominated by the fact that what we were there to celebrate was not just us, but us as a Christian couple. And it was almost like coming out as a Christian, you know as well as, and as a gay Christian, as well as, which a lot of people think of as a contradiction.

In summary, for queer theologians like Stuart, gender and sexual identities are deconstructed through baptismal incorporation into the Body of Christ. Whereas the research participants may not all have rejected fixed understandings of identity, they all hint at a wider and more deeply felt identity in Christ than that provided by their sex or gender, and this identity they understand themselves to share with the whole community of Church.

However, another equally important line of development in queer theology was explored by Marcella Althaus-Reid, whose work Stuart understands as liberation theology informed by queer theology rather than queer theology itself. Althaus-Reid uses queer theory as a tool to analyse experience, certainly, but in her work human experience remains primary. Althaus-Reid writes, in considering the ways in which queer discourses are silenced: 'We live in a theological world where God is known by gossip – by elite gossip' (2003, p.49). She calls herself 'a material girl' and queer theology a materialist theology that takes bodies seriously: 'The search for love and for truth is a bodily one. Bodies in love add many theological insights to the quest for God and truth' (p.2).

She begins with the human experience of bodily love in the same way that liberation theologians began theology for social transformation with the work of members of politically and economically oppressed communities. Examining this experience, she defines queer theology as first-person theology that is in 'diaspora' or 'exile', and that is self-disclosing, autobiographical and responsible for its own words. What I saw in Kitaj resonates with a diaspora theology, at a crossroads of issues of self-identity and the identity of the Christian community. I am seeking in my writing the 'biographies of sexual migrants, testimonies of real lives in rebellious modes of love, pleasure and suffering' (Althaus-Reid 2003, p.8). Althaus-Reid does not require that queer theology disregard Church traditions but suggests a process of queering that may turn them upside-down, or submit them to collage-style processes, and that search for and add experiences that may have been excluded and ignored.

This process of queering un-shapes and re-shapes traditional theology by questioning at all times and in all ways its heterosexual hermeneutic. How does it do this? By inserting into theology stories of transgressive life and culture. Such stories disturb us to be honest ourselves, to admit the sheer complexity and diverse nature of all our sexual experience and consequent identity.

Althaus-Reid's queer theology begins not with theology but with bodies. The stories of the research participants include stories of acknowledged sexual attraction and desire. With that attraction many of the stories of healing and liberation begin. Here Christina describes how the strength of such desire broke through a heavy sense of taboo:

> *Discovering that I had highly sexual and loving feelings for another woman, and not having recognized that or named it until an explosion of recognition which burst through that blanket covering which I think I had thrown over that unacceptable set of longings and desires. Feeling both ecstatic and agonizingly self-doubting at the same time.*

Emma recognizes her partner's beauty at the service she describes with utter conviction as her wedding:

> *We just had barely slept. We had to get up in the middle of the night and have a cold bath [laughing]. We had this room at the top of a hotel, and there was no air conditioning. It was just so uncomfortable and sticky, so morning came and we got dressed and F was wearing a really pretty – it looked like a dress but it was really a skirt and a bodice and the bodice was all embroidered with little tiny pearls and things. Her stepmother had made it. And her skirt, none of us realized until the day that it was slightly transparent [laughing] so with the sun behind you could really see her lovely legs... It was a nice moment.*

Yet Emma, who describes herself as gender queer, also acknowledges the awkwardness of bodies, the difficulty in dressing to express who we are, and the sheer discomfort involved for some of us in dressing for the performed occasion:

> *And I was wearing a sort of silk suit from Monsoon with a waistcoat and it ended up being too hot to wear the jacket for most of the day. And I am not sure we would do that quite like that now. Cos it felt, you know, even at the time it felt like we are going to be put into assumed gender roles that are other people's stuff. And my understanding of gender has moved on in the last 20 years even you know, but even then I felt like, 'So, I'm the man, I'm the groom'. Even one of our friends' husbands said to me on the day, 'It's tough being the groom.' Um, and I didn't really have the words to say, 'I'm not the groom'. And I am not 'the bride' either!*

Lucy is clear about the strength of her physical and emotional desire to bear children as a strong motivation to enter a civil partnership:

> *Well, my partner and I met on the internet, so, er, the last two relationships I had been in had been really manky, really, and just hard work. So, it was, to me, like, 'This is who I am, and this is what I want.' There's no kind of emotion involved in the initial stages, so people that don't want a kid, well just, 'Go away then, I don't need you for me.'*

For most research participants the first experience of relationship was of longed-for love fulfilled by another human being, before a deepened understanding of the love of God was kindled, as Christina movingly describes here:

> *I think I am fundamentally altered by this whole experience, so that my faith and values and worldview are not the same. So yes, I think it leads me to be profoundly grateful and my faith is changed by that. That instead of having a sense of incompleteness and craving in life, um, where my faith would be partly trying to resolve those questions, this gives me a much, I suppose really such a profound sense of love that my understanding of the love of God is deeply influenced by it.*

These stories raise the disturbing question of what happens when this reflex to love is suppressed by the self, or constrained by others. Even more painful is the question of how participants who knew violence or the threat of violence as they grew up as a direct result of their sexual orientation would be healed without the physical and emotional love of another fully expressed in a long-term, committed relationship. Matthew speaks movingly of such healing:

> *...in the relationship I was personally working on a lot of neurosis with my partner, and he being supportive. And I think my role to him is similar as well.*

Matthew is clear that only later was he overwhelmed with the sense of the Holy Spirit's presence in this relationship:

> *So, I notice that the stuff which is put in front of me to work on after our marriage is different, is of a different type or flavour. Um, so I could sense a sense of purpose of what God is asking us to do through marriage.*

Another participant, Sue, glimpsed this queer activity of God in her strong sense of the presence of God experienced where Church and state both dictated that God was not to be named in her civil partnership celebration:

> Obviously on the day itself you can't use anything religious in the ceremony, although we did our best. We used two pieces of music, one referring to being with this person in the Promised Land, and we had quasi-religious poems and another song – as long as you don't say God – and our view is that God was there anyway. If you believe that God's here, in the room, and everywhere, then God was present at our civil ceremony even though He wasn't supposed to be. We said our promises both when we said them to ourselves with our rings, and when we said them to the registrar, it was in front of the registrar and God, in our hearts.

Her story reminds us of a God who acts in ways contrary to our expectations, who is afraid neither of difference nor of conflict. Matthew wanted to recall this God in a reading at the service of prayer and dedication following his civil partnership:

> Do you think I came to bring peace on earth? No, I tell you, but division. From now on there will be five in one family divided against each other, three against two and two against three. They will be divided, father against son and son against father, mother against daughter and daughter against mother, mother-in-law against daughter-in-law and daughter-in-law against mother-in-law. (Luke 12:51–53)

Liberation theology and the Church, Althaus-Reid argues, need to listen to and honour such stories of liberation, which begin with queer bodies, and to discern in them God's activities of healing and blessing.

The uses of queer theology

Before investigating the ways in which I have used queer theology in this book, it is first important for me to add three points of clarification about what I am attempting to do by its use.

First, having immersed myself in the accounts of my research participants, as I endeavour to interpret the meanings they gave to their relationships, it is my interpretation, not theirs, that here there is queer theology. Of the 13 people interviewed, only two use the word *queer* and only one the words *queer theology*. Nonetheless, it is precisely because they are gay and lesbian, enjoying 'transgressive relationships', and within that place are experiencing and journeying with God, that I ultimately call the theology they create queer.

Second, in calling God 'queer', I speak of human language about God, not of the being of God-self, since I cannot and do not claim to know that God-self in Him/Herself. I may believe that I know queer revelations of God, and as a Christian experience the queer revelation of God in Jesus of Nazareth, crucified as an outlaw outside the city wall. Yet to know God is not to point to, know or possess an object – that is idolatry – but is instead a way to describe putting myself into the hands of unknowable mystery, who is to be worshipped, explored and related to dynamically in Christ. This 'not knowing' of God is an essential aspect of traditional theology restated by its new, wayward, queer offspring. Queerness cannot be easily pinned down and may indeed open the way to an apophatic understanding of God.[3] The theologian Gerard Loughlin reminds us how this new queer thought is borrowed, from and traceable within the Christian tradition: 'God's being is indubitable but radically unknowable, and any theology that forgets this is undeniably straight, not queer' (2007, p.10). We cannot say what God is, or what queer is. We can instead point to queer theology's activity of leading us beyond present understandings and definitions of what it is to be God, and what it is to be human.

Third, when I gave this chapter the title 'Something Borrowed, Something New', I thought initially of what theologies of civil partnership would borrow from traditional Christian theologies of marriage, recalling the wedding rhyme that a bride should wear 'Something old, something new, something borrowed, something blue'. Queer theology, however, is present throughout Christian

---

3   The apophatic view of God relates to God's utter transcendence, remoteness and unknowableness. This view of God lives in tension for Christian believers with the kataphatic view, which emphasizes the many ways in which God may be known by human beings.

history, yet brings new insights to the table of a theology of human relationships for the early third millennium. It is indeed something both old and new, simultaneously.

A queer understanding of the presence of God: Queer sacramental theology

In understanding the relationships of my research participants to be sacramental in nature, I interpreted God's presence to be experienced in secular as well as sacred life circumstances and events. Gay and lesbian Christians, describing an awareness of the divine in their relationships of transgressive love, heal disconnections in our interpretations of our human experiences of love and of God between body and spirit, earth and heaven, eroticism and prayerfulness, faithfulness and aberrancy, the sacred and the profane. Queer theology finds this healing of dualism to be at the heart of the Hebrew and Christian Scriptures, sensing there a God who is present in rebellion and diversity as much as in propriety and order. In God's salvation history, the person chosen by God to lead Israel is the rascal Jacob, the woman chosen to save Israel is the harlot Rahab who is an ancestor of Jesus of Nazareth, and later the first theologian apostle to the Gentiles is Paul, a mass murderer of Christians. To stretch our theological imagination further, as Graham Ward suggests, the new creation of the world, in the incarnation of Christ, necessarily destabilizes our traditional categories of human gender, let alone our gendered interpretations of God:

> The baby boy is husband and bridegroom, spouse and refigured love of the other who gives him birth, whose own body swells to contain the future Church. The bridal chamber is the womb which the bridegroom will impregnate with his seed while also being the womb from which he emerges. The material orders are inseparable from the solid and transcendent orders, the orders of mystery... And so here Jesus' body is brought within a complex network of sexualised symbolic relations that confound incest and the sacred. (1999, pp.164–165)

Many theologians have combed Christian theology, including sacramental theology, to find a queer God. For Graham Ward, the body of Christ is queer, and Christians are incorporated into this queer body in the Eucharist, sharing in its sacramental flesh (1999, p.176). Eugene Rogers emphasizes baptism, in which we are incorporated into the death of Christ, and made a new creation, to deconstruct the whole notion of what we understand by 'the natural' (1999, p.65). Stuart's understanding of this grace of God leads her to insist that it is our baptismal identity that usefully subverts all sexual and gender identities. She perceives this subversion to be queer theology's greatest contribution to Christian theology, demonstrating how sexual and gender identities 'are constructed in the context of power and are part of a matrix of dominance and exclusion' (2007, p.68).

Another theological concept enjoyed by queer theologians for its gender fluid symbolism is the Trinity, described here by Rogers:

God as the Trinity, without reference to persons can, in traditional Christian exegesis, both require masculine pronouns and can be our 'Mother'; God is Father but not male; Jesus is Mother but not female; the Spirit is male, female, or neuter, depending on language, and also denied to have gender. (1999, p.197)

Stuart (2007) ends 'Sacramental Flesh', a chapter concerning these queer sacramental presences of God in *Queer Theology: Rethinking the Western Body*, with a consideration of the sacramental nature of death itself. In death we experience the final destruction of our sexual and gendered identity, yet our source of hope remains in our being initiated into the paschal mystery of Christ in our baptism: 'All bonds, associations and worldly achievements pale into insignificance beside the status of the deceased as a baptized member of the body of Christ' (p.74).

To summarize, Ward, Stuart and Rogers demonstrate myriad ways in which queer sacramental theology has developed as a conceptual tool, deconstructing all categories of gender and sexual identity by appeal to traditional theology. Stuart pushes this method of deconstruction to its ultimate conclusion: 'The Church is the only community under a direct mandate to be queer, and it is only within the Church that queer theory reaches its telos' (2007, p.75). She continues:

> Queer flesh is sacramental flesh nudging the queer performer towards the eschatological horizon and sacramental flesh is queer flesh nudging the Christian towards the realisation that in Christ maleness and femaleness and gay and straight are categories that dissolve before the throne of grace where only the garment of baptism remains. (p.75)

In the context of my own life and research, this direction in queer theology, this understanding of what it means to be a sign of God's queer presence, renders me uneasy. My research participants believed that they both were, and had seen, signs of God's love in their relationship. Yet the relationship was first experienced as a desire of heart and body for another human person. What seems missing in this development of queer sacramental theology is emphasis on queer bodies, relating in strange circumstances, to a God who is larger and stranger than the God of the Church, and who delivers gay and lesbian Christians from that Church's oppressive mechanisms of inclusion and exclusion. I seek a queer sacramental theology that honours 'the complex human web' (Miller-McLemore 1993, p.367, p.369) of embodied relationships rather than smoothing over the potentially wild diversity of gender and sexual difference in which God may be known. I seek God's face in ungraceful circumstances, and God's voice outside the constraints of traditional Christian worship.

I am urged to spread a wide net to capture signs of God's presence by remembering moments in my ministry in Soho. Following the murder of a gay man, a young dancer/choreographer, who worshipped with us, worked with bodies from parish and community to create a stage play of grief and resistance to homophobia at the Soho Theatre. Was that not a sacrament? When the London Gay Men's Chorus yelled out the gay hymn 'Over the Rainbow' in their love at the death of yet another friend from the AIDS virus, was that not a sacramental moment? Was God not present there in feather boa, make-up and lament? My research participants recalled similar non-church sacramental moments: bodies, both gay and straight, nuns and lay-people, trying to figure out which dancing column to join at a post-wedding barn dance; two men wearing 'Just Married' sashes at a Gay Pride March, where for once Christians were applauded not jeered; or simply moments of admitting God's presence in the silent worship of devout hearts at a civil partnership ceremony.

The God of these queer sacraments does not need obedience framed in orthodox Christian language. One research participant was freed from the oppressive constraints of 'guilt' and 'sin' by gradually losing faith in the God of Christianity, and indeed in any belief in God; another was revolted as a feminist by the idea of alignment of self with the death of Christ; while another thrives in the community of a gay and lesbian protest church.

I seek a broader direction of travel for queer sacramental theology since sacramental language, which so reinforces the power and position of Church in human life, is too often not resonant for me with the experience of, and quest for, human liberation for gay and lesbian people.

A queer understanding of the activity of God: Queer liberation theology

The theologian David Ford notes that improvisation around a theme is essential to living the Christian faith, which

> is true to itself only by becoming freshly embodied in different contexts... Theologically understood, they (such improvisations) are testimony to God's creativity and abundance... They show the particular activity of the Holy Spirit – a flourishing of distinctive and different realisations of the eventfulness of God. (1999, p.144)

Marcella Althaus-Reid stretches our imaginative vision of God's 'eventfulness' by seeing the living God in transgressive love experienced outside, as well as inside, the linguistic and social contexts of church. Althaus-Reid seeks a radically queer and relational God, incarnate in every human life, who refuses to stand over against human bodies and stories in search of God. She does this to provoke us to see that unless God is understood outside the constraints of human propriety and construction, God's otherness will always be negated. In my research findings, I identified this queer God in civil partnership rites where God was not permitted, officially, to be mentioned, yet who was named 'secretly' by Christian worshippers who were not permitted to have their relationships blessed in church. I glimpsed this queer God, too, in relationships which had flourished in faithful love for many years outside the support of family, Church and state.

A second reason for my unease over queer theologies that are almost entirely ecclesiastically framed is a suspicion that, while they form the basis for theological reflection, and are, in this sense, very important, there is no sign that they create a basis for increased political awareness or action towards those who are both sexually and economically marginal. Rather than in the abstracted arguments of queer theory and theology, research participants had instead found liberation in the increased tolerance towards homosexuality in secular society, which had culminated in the demand for the legal recognition of same-sex partnerships. Their lives had been improved by the work of activists agitating for greater social equality for lesbian and gay people over years. In this political process, and its results for them personally, they experienced the liberating activity of God.

In *Queering Theology* (2004, p.2) Althaus-Reid and Isherwood claim that queer theology is essentially about love. Like the participants in this research, they are keen to explore how individuals and societies can act more lovingly. Just as love prompts questions about the morality of systems and language that receive theological sanction, so queer theology is of little use if it does not engage with the sexual and gender oppression of those, like my research participants, whose identities do not fit theologically approved patterns of relating. How do these queer liberation theologians avoid the trap of making queer theology merely discursive on the one hand, or militantly exclusive in its opposition to certain phenomena on the other? Althaus-Reid suggests that queer theology should proceed via a variety of different political acts, rather than set up another line of binary opposition. In the queer liberation theology that I perceive in these research findings, participants act politically for justice and healing in society in multiple ways, locally, nationally and internationally, in ecology, in mental health, in theology, in family life, in church and in LGBTQ activism. They do this in response to the energy and security they receive in relationships of transgressive love.

This is queer theology

In terms of content, this book is itself queer theology, a gathering of stories about bodily love from people who themselves even in recent history have often been dismissed as not Christian, not able to reflect on God. The queer theology of Elizabeth Stuart, which addresses questions of identity, suggests powerfully that in Christ homosexuality and heterosexuality, like maleness and femaleness, are categories that dissolve before the throne of grace where 'only the garment of baptism remains' (2003, p.75). The queer theology of Marcella Althaus-Reid, which addresses questions of human relating, claims that queer theology is essentially about love (Althaus-Reid and Isherwood 2004). Just as love prompts questions about the morality of systems and language that receive theological sanction, so queer theology is of little use if it does not engage with the sexual and gender oppression of those whose identities do not fit theologically approved patterns of relating. What of the relationships described in this book? Is this a queer form of marriage, or not?

Chapter 5

ENDURING LOVE

Is This Marriage or Not?

> *My image [of civil partnership] is of something permanent,*
> *something strongly planted in the landscape, like a tree, which*
> *has been growing for a long time and which will stay there for*
> *many years to come.*

David (research participant)

David suggests that civil partnership is an open, public commitment to create an enduring lifelong relationship of love with another person. For nearly all the research participants, both as a rite and a relationship, it represents a significant step, a sacramental moment, a realization of God's work of liberation in their lives. Why, then, confuse the significant project of civil partnership, the subject of my original research, with the equally weighty project of marriage?

As I planned this research project in 2010, I did not intend to link civil partnership with same-sex marriage, unless it became clear that research participants themselves explicitly made that connection. I changed my intention, however, for four reasons. First, the media had found early civil partnerships, especially among 'celebrities', newsworthy, and had instantly labelled them 'gay weddings'. The imagery of marriage had therefore rapidly surrounded the rite. Then, two years later, as I began my interviews, the Government Equalities Office published the Equal Marriage Consultation, a widely disseminated consultation paper on same-sex marriage (Government Equalities Office 2012). This consultation prepared the way for Royal Assent to be given in July 2013 to the Marriage (Same Sex Couples) Bill, and for the first same-sex marriages to take place in England and Wales in March 2014. Third, the alignment of civil partnership and marriage was quickly made by pilot research participants in their responses to my questions. Finally, whereas few theologians had written about civil partnership, books, papers and conferences about the theology of gay marriage, already popular in the US, for example in the work of Goss (1993), Hefling (1996), Rogers (1999, 2002) and Loughlin (2007), began to appear in the UK. Among the early authors in the UK writing about same-sex marriage were the theologians Stuart (2003) and Alison (2001, 2002, 2010). More recently, there have followed the Church of England senior clergy John (2012) and Wilson (2014), and the theologians Coakley (2013, 2015), Song (2014) and Hensman (2015). In 2016, the theologian Andrew Davison and the leading evangelical campaigner for gay equality Jayne Ozanne edited and published collections of writings to be read by members of the General Synod of the Church of England for debate in July of that year (Davison 2016; Ozanne 2016).

I nevertheless encountered within myself resistance to making this conflation of meanings so soon. As I began writing this chapter, before completing it, I took a serious fall. Fainting at the kitchen sink, I hit my head so hard that I was concussed for a month and could not write. At the time, I made no connection between this incident and my attempt to write this chapter. But as I returned to the chapter, and to the question in its title, I experienced again the power of this resistance, and knew that I must examine it for this chapter to be authentic.

The swift alignment between civil partnership and marriage was made by the research participants in their interviews in three clear ways. First, the words *marriage* or *wedding* were used at some point in the interview, whether fleetingly or deliberately, by ten of the 13 participants to describe the ceremony or celebration of their civil partnership *before* I asked a direct question about its likeness to marriage. Second, even where the words *marriage* or *wedding* were not used, or used very fleetingly, civil partnership celebrations were clearly resonant of marriage celebrations. In all cases, families and friends were invited or informed; in all cases, special clothes were purchased and luxurious food eaten; in all cases, special photographs were taken and hotels or other smart venues used in preparation or celebration; in many cases, speeches were made, hairdressers visited, flowers arranged, and so on. Third, halfway through each interview, I introduced a question about the likeness of civil partnership to marriage, thereby opening the debate explicitly with participants.

At first, I imagined my resistance to this swift alignment of meanings to spring from my need to digest new ideas and possibilities slowly – a slowness I described in the last chapter, where I started to explore queer theology. Would it not have been useful to experience civil partnership for some decades in order to have time to explore the specific contours of gay and lesbian long-term relationships? Perhaps I sensed it made us – myself included – 'special'? I had been looking forward to examining these contours of difference in this research. However, the resistance to the alignment stemmed from more painful roots. The Bishops of the Church of England had been very cautious about clergy entering civil partnerships, but it was not forbidden. To enter a same-sex civil marriage was, by contrast, forbidden, and if I were to do so I would run the risk of losing a licence to minister. The House of Bishops Pastoral Statement written in response to the same-sex marriage legislation clearly states that clergy are not to enter same-sex marriage, not to bless such marriages, or to use church buildings to do so (Church of England 2014).

Since writing well involves the assimilation and consideration of others' ideas, writing about civil partnership understood by my research participants to be marriage would entail either my inner, possibly dishonest, denial of the appeal and importance of such ideas, or my envisaging for this group something of value that I myself cannot have. Writing necessitated confronting my decision to place my priesthood within the Church of England before my partnership, something I had managed successfully to avoid so far. To write this chapter was to be aware of pain and to find ways of reflecting safely about that pain. It is no wonder, perhaps, that I fell, vomiting up that which was indigestible, broke my head, and injured my brain, since to go on using my brain was possibly too painful to contemplate for a while. I needed time for reflection.

Having examined that resistance, and discovered that the research is itself a method of coming to terms by reading and reflection, with the meaning of being Christian and lesbian, in civil partnership and a priest in the Church of England, I am able to set the scene for this chapter. I begin by stating the obvious, that civil partnership may be understood as a social construction that permits a relationship to be framed and shaped in particular ways. I then examine the layers of meaning and experience contained within this framework. I find that research participants are confused over whether this framework is essentially that of marriage or not. I establish that 11 of the 13 participants wish to be married, and that they understand civil partnership relationally, if not legally and linguistically, to be marriage. Examining the meaning of marriage as it is expounded in the introduction to the marriage service in the Church of England prayer book *Common Worship*, I identify which aspects of marriage participants wish to retain and re-interpret from a queer theological perspective, and which they wish to challenge or reject. Having created a list of identifiable marks of marriage as so understood, I suggest that, far from weakening the meaning of marriage, the experience of faithful committed same-sex relationships may expand our understanding of marriage in useful and theologically rich ways.

Social constructions of civil partnership
Supporting lifelong mutual commitment

Vanessa, an interviewee, uses a striking picture by Rothko, the painting 'Light, Earth and Blue',[1] displayed on her laptop during the interview with me, to describe levels and layers of meaning in her relationship of civil partnership. She understands civil partnership primarily as an enduring framework for her relationship. Sometimes she and her partner act as frames of containment for each other, while sometimes they are the colours within the frame that holds them:

> Sometimes Alice is one of the block colours, and she is allowed to go
> deeper and deeper into whatever she's going through, and I act as the

1   See note 1, Chapter 2.

> *frame around her, like holding her safe. Or I can be the backdrop... But it's difficult to focus on all three colours at once, because when you see it in the flesh it's over four metres high. So, the eye is constantly shifting, and re-focusing, trying to understand the different perspectives of the space which has been created, which is what Mark Rothko is I think trying to do. And I think that's similar to our relationship, because I can't look at my relationship with Alice from just one angle. I am always shifting my perspective because it has been built on so many layers and levels.*

All 13 participants stress the paradigm of faithful committed relationship as the most essential element in this framework. At first, this may appear to be a simple copying of heteronormative behaviour and values. Emma suggests that when she participated in her wedding, as she called her civil partnership rite, she was simply following established patterns of pursuit, courtship and marriage, while Ted admits that he wants to be married as his parents were. But on further reflection, participants give their own reasons for wanting such commitment, based on their own experience of relationships so far. Ted explains this in his own terms, which are associated with re-evaluation counselling:

> *I think that for me the paradigm, the image, is committed relationship. And that means – one of the important parts of our relationship is that we are both involved in a counselling project, right? Co-counselling, re-evaluation counselling, whatever you want to call it. And it has helped me a lot. It's a spiritual practice. So part of that spiritual practice is the idea that when you are committed to somebody, when you love somebody, a lot of stuff will come up. Right, so let's get to work on stuff! Right? So, that makes sense to me. And my working on my stuff together with him is like the overarching idea of what's going on.*

Christina holds a psychological belief in the importance of permanence as a core value in the relationship:

> *I have experienced and believe that for a relationship of love of this kind to flourish and thrive it needs to be secure and not subject to*

> cruel or unnecessary anxieties about whether it will be maintained and whether there would be any risk of relationships or dalliances or ending the relationship because it was going through some difficulties, and that a commitment to continuing the relationship through inevitable difficulties is the best way to secure and maintain it as a secure base for mutual flourishing.

All participants are convinced of the importance of the legal aspect of this framework. Its status in law provides for mutual love and responsibility to be earthed in the practical outworking of shared care for the other in terms of finance, property and citizenship provision. For Lucy, shared housing and the shared parenting of her child became possible with civil partnership. For Ted's partner, the right to remain in the UK was afforded by civil partnership. All participants are convinced too, as explained more fully in Chapter 2, of the importance of the social recognition afforded by the framework of civil partnership.

Among the participants, only one, Lucy, voiced that she understood one advantage of this social construction to be that it was new, and that she and her partner could therefore 'do with it what they wanted', untrammelled by tradition. This newness was a disadvantage, however, for Matthew, who needs the older framework of marriage to gain social recognition in his home country:

> I know how civil partnership is being ridiculed in my country. It's not taken seriously. If I say to my homophobic friends there that I am in a civil partnership then they are likely to respond back, 'Yeah, that is one of those things that you do in the Western world.' But if I say that I am married and show them my marriage certificate, then I would be taken seriously, I think.

The principle disadvantage of this framework for 11 of the 13 participants is that it lacks the equality with heterosexual relationships that marriage would provide.

'Am I married?'

Anne is confused. Following her rite of civil partnership, is she married or not? Her lesbian and gay friends assume that she is married. Her partner, albeit in affectionate jest, sometimes calls her 'wife'. She feels that she is married. On the other hand, many family members still address her as 'Miss' and her mother-in-law, to whom she is very close, acknowledges her as a daughter-in-law in private, but in public as her daughter's 'friend'. She says:

> One of the things I get very cross about is that it's seen as marriage by all our friends but it's not marriage for our families, I don't think. I'm constantly having to reaffirm with some member of my family that it's a real relationship.

She longs to be married in church, so will settle for no less in the shape of either an equal same-sex civil marriage ceremony, or a church service of prayer and dedication for a civil partnership:

> Really what we want to do and what we have always wanted to do is get married in church, not just being tolerated and not just having a blessing but having a full marriage in church.

Yet she imagines the possibility of a church wedding to lie a long way off, and possibly not to exist within the span of her lifetime. She clearly understands her civil partnership to be the nearest rite of legal recognition she could obtain to marriage:

> It's marriage for me because it's all we can do.

Stephen places this confusion squarely in the minds of onlookers rather than in his own mind. While he and his partner will certainly get married, as an act of solidarity with all those who have worked for equal same-sex marriage, he understands himself, through his civil partnership and church service of prayer and dedication, to be married already. He uses words to describe his marriage status to fit the circumstances, preferring not to offend:

> I think of it as the wedding...it is dependent on whom I am talking to. So, people who were present, and who may not have a particularly complex theological agenda...would call that a wedding. And I call it our wedding... Then again, to people of a certain younger generation who are comfortable with the concept of gay marriage I would call it a wedding. I would be careful sometimes to call it a blessing or a thanksgiving service to people who I think may have a particularly nuanced approach to it.

Lillian is convinced that she is married. She understands the rite of civil partnership to have acted as the legal completion of a marriage that took place at a church service of blessing many years ago in 1995. The rite of civil partnership is for her the delayed signing of a register stating that she is married.

Two participants show no sign of unease or confusion over whether they are married for opposite reasons. They neither seek to be married, nor believe that their relationship is one of marriage. Robert says:

> For us a civil partnership is ideal: it is not marriage but confers all the rights and responsibilities of a marriage...traditional marriage suits some people. It's not for us.

Gradually, in the transcripts, a picture emerges of whether participants understand their relationships to be marriage, or not. Christina clarifies this picture by making a distinction between relational understanding and linguistic and legal understandings of marriage. She suggests:

> I think in relationship terms it has the same meaning as marriage... being a publicly stated commitment to an exclusive relationship intended to be lifelong to another person, where the purpose is to provide to that other person love and companionship, um, in order to support that person in a relationship of the fullness of love.

However, she is clear that it does not have exactly the same civic, legal or linguistic status as marriage:

> *And I think in many important respects it represents the same commitments and underlying purposes as marriage but precisely because it isn't called marriage, isn't legally marriage, I think it is not the same as marriage. It does not have the same civic, legal or linguistic status as marriage.*

Civil partnership represents a step in the progress towards equality for these research participants. For all but the two who are content with the civil partnership relationship status, it represents, as Anne describes it, as 'the best [they] could do'.

The importance of equality

Queer theology began in gay and lesbian theology. These theologies took an essentialist view of human sexuality, arguing that being gay is part of God's created order. They followed and reflected on the movement for gay and lesbian equality, which was precipitated in 1969 when New York police raided the Stonewall bar, and gays and lesbians fought back. Mary Hunt describes the significance of this new movement: 'No longer were same-sex relationships simply the stuff of back rooms and Mafia-run bars. Homosexuals were persons with dignity and (eventually) legal rights equal to all others' (Hunt 1991). In 1974, in an early work in gay and lesbian liberation theology, *Loving Women/Loving Men: Gay Liberation and the Church*, Gearhart and Johnson argued that marriage is a covenant relationship and that such a relationship is available to people of any gender. In 1977, in *Towards a Theology of Gay Liberation*, the Christian sociologist Malcolm Macourt outlined a gay liberationist vision for young people who

> will become aware of a wide variety of life patterns: monogamy – multiple partnerships; partnerships for life – partnerships for a period of mutual growth; same-sex partners – opposite partners – both; chastity; living in community – living in small family units... The goal of the Christian gay liberationists must be that the choice of pattern which makes most sense to each and every person will be seen most clearly to allow them to accord with the

injunctions: 'love the Lord your God with all your heart, with all your soul, with all your mind, and with all your strength' and 'love your neighbour as yourself' (Mark 12:30). (1977, pp.24–25)

Influenced by the gay liberation movement, participants suggested different motivations for wanting the equality of marriage. Three were personally affronted at standing out as possessing a relationship of civil partnership, making the point that in effect they are 'outed' by the knowledge of their relationship status, as Vanessa exclaims:

> Why should we stick out like a sore thumb? I know that our love is just as genuine and as beautiful as the next heterosexual couple. There's nothing wrong in it, and I just feel like we are being labelled.

Two participants gave theological justification for being treated equally, Ted arguing from a gay liberationist standpoint and David from the diversity of God's human creation all created in God's image. Ten gave political reasons. Lillian expresses the longing to be in solidarity with other campaigners, including those concerned for universal human rights for gay and lesbian people:

> I volunteer at a large LGBT charity, and so many people put their backs into this so that in register offices at least gay people can say they are married. Then you don't have to tick on a form 'civil partnership', and it's different, and you know with countries that are leaving the Commonwealth and want to treat gay people as second-class citizens and with what's happening in Russia, I feel proud the Brits are doing it.

Meanwhile, Stephen suggests that to begin to use the language of marriage for civil partnership may eventually lead to progress in equality:

> I don't want to concede that point to the Church, in a sense, and myself start calling it 'not a wedding'. There is a lot of good reason why we would want to call it a 'gay wedding' because that's what happened with civil partnerships! People called them 'gay weddings' and then suddenly everyone, including apparently the Bishops in the House of

> *Lords, thinks that civil partnerships are great! And the populace at large think they are tantamount to marriage! So, you know, I think there is a lot of power in language that we underestimate.*

Action for equality, together with being bound together with other gay and lesbian people in protest, is one way of coping with the pressures of belonging to a heteronormative culture. Stephen is clear about this pressure to belong to a heteronormative culture, which he understands as a benign influence in his life:

> *There are two different influences. You know, there are the straight married friends of ours who have children who are very much part of our lives – including those we share a house with outside London – they are in stable long-term marriages, and they are our social circle in London. They are a positive influence and example. On the other hand, we have other friends who are single or gay friends who are in open relationships, we know other sorts of relationships out there who would almost pull you in a different direction.*

There are signs in these interviews of participants being sensitive towards other types of relationship, and of not wishing to impose their own choices on those not wishing or able to live as a couple. Lillian humorously indicated awareness of this tension:

> *I am really aware that not everybody that's gay or bi or queer or trans is in a relationship. And not everybody wants to be. And some people are in more complicated to define relationships. I have an acquaintance who lives with two partners, one male, one female... When she was describing it, I thought this was quite a challenge for me, because it's quite straight to be married isn't it? [laughs]*

As this chapter unfolds it will become clearer whether equality means for this group being the same as their heterosexual counterparts, or different but equal. In the following section, I examine the Christian theology of marriage as presently expounded in the Church of England marriage service to identify where this theology is accepted and where challenged, expanded, or rejected in the queer marriage theology of the research participants.

A queer theology of marriage

The introduction to the service of marriage in *Common Worship*, the Church of England prayer book, contains these words:[2]

Marriage is a gift of God in creation
through which husband and wife may know the grace of God.
It is given
that as man and woman grow together in love and trust,
they shall be united with one another in heart, body and mind,
as Christ is united with his bride, the Church.

The gift of marriage brings husband and wife together
in the delight and tenderness of sexual union
and joyful commitment to the end of their lives.
It is given as the foundation of family life
in which children are [born and] nurtured
and in which each member of the family, in good times and in bad,
may find strength, companionship and comfort,
and grow to maturity in love.

Marriage is a way of life made holy by God,
and blessed by the presence of our Lord Jesus Christ
with those celebrating a wedding at Cana in Galilee.
Marriage is a sign of unity and loyalty
which all should uphold and honour.
It enriches society and strengthens community.
No one should enter into it lightly or selfishly
but reverently and responsibly in the sight of almighty God.

---

2   The text of the marriage service can be found at www.churchofengland. org/prayer-and-worship/worship-texts-and-resources/common-worship/ marriage

Which elements in this introduction do participants retain in their own theology of marriage and which do they modify as a result of their own queer experience of lifelong committed intimate relationships?

A gift of God in creation

There is no sign of participants understanding marriage as a creation ordinance, a commandment of God that can be read into our story from the beginning of creation. Rather, they understand it as a human institution changing in its nature and emphasis through history, as Stephen describes:

> I think marriage as an institution is very much conformed and shaped by the society in which it exists... I would think that as a society we have come such a long way, that the institution of marriage more generally has been liberalized and become much more of a sort of equal union.

If they allude to the creation narratives of the biblical book of Genesis, they point to God's diverse creation, as David does:

> Creation is quite important to me in two ways. One is that we are all God's children. We are all created in the image of God. And essentially because I know what is good within me and what is not, I have never had a moral or a religious problem with my sexuality. That goes back to my creation as a child of God in the image of God as we all are.

He uses his experience in a queer way, to test biblical texts and Church history for truthfulness to that experience:

> What I don't believe is that literally on the sixth day God created man and the animals. Really, that's a very good image to remind us to be careful when we read Scripture and to question the experience through, to some extent, our own feelings, and through the history of the Church as well, what is right and what isn't. And to test those things by what we know of God and the love of God.

Lucy's theology is less formally articulated than that of David, but unconsciously she paints a word picture of her civil partnership celebration, as if she and Sarah were in Eden, when she shows me beautiful photographs of herself and her partner in two light, matched summer dresses with sashes as they walk in deep countryside. There are flowers on the dresses and they both look entirely natural, part of the natural world:

> The picture that I sort of think of when I think about our civil partnership are these pictures where we are kind of walking through the fields, and kind of away, and in the trees. This is how I feel about it...it's kind of like there's no real possessions going on here, we're just together, and out in a field.

Only one participant uses the interview to question the essential nature of gender, certain that she possesses both male and female characteristics sufficient to understand herself as 'gender queer'. Twelve participants believe their gender as male or female to be given, like their sexual orientation. If God has so created them, same-sex attraction is also part of that creation.

People living in same-sex relationships, however, also know the attraction and tension of living with difference. These differences are highlighted in terms of temperament, gift, skill, personal faith and family background. David highlights a common theme, that difference brings life to these relationships:

> I recognize, very much, the differences between us, and it's the way we spark off each other that amongst other things makes our relationship a good one, I think.

Ted deepens further our understanding of the importance of living with difference:

> Like, I tend to be surprised when I actually – I used to do this a lot earlier in my life when really my life was a lot about me and I didn't pay as much attention to other people – I would occasionally be surprised

> that the other person was actually a different person than I thought
> that they were.

He spoke of coming to terms with profound differences between himself and his partner in terms of age, race and economic status, and of his partner sometimes acting as an uncomfortable mirror to his own unconscious prejudices.

Emerging in their understanding of complementing each other in difference are ideas and concepts close to those explored by Anthony Giddens in *The Transformation of Intimacy* (1992). In this work, Giddens suggests we are participants in a sexual revolution. His argument is clustered around three main concepts: *sexuality which is plastic*, the *pure relationship*, and *confluent love*. Sexuality which is plastic is sexuality severed from integration with reproduction. It is loosed from pre-ordained shapes, from having meaning within bonds of kinship and intergenerational care by being reified, becoming a possession of the individual. A pure relationship refers to a situation where a social relation is entered into for its own sake, for what can be derived by each person from a sustained relationship with another. Confluent love demands less acceptance of the romantic idea of one gender lacking what is present in the opposite gender, so requiring a marriage partner of the opposite sex to fulfil a gap or lack. It emphasizes instead a willingness to give equally within a relationship, especially in terms of self-communication and sexual relating.

Experiencing equality, or the struggle to achieve a sense of equality, is a vital part of these relationships. There is a refusal to accept gender-typical roles, although this is verbalized more by the female participants than the male. Vanessa is determined to overturn the gendered roles she sees her heterosexual friends adopting:

> We are at the age where a lot of our friends are getting married. I just
> don't understand why women take the man's name. And that really
> upsets me. All my friends, except one person. Also, among my friends
> there are some quite strong-minded people. Yet, when it comes down to
> things like daily tasks and things like that, I find that my female friends
> will do the majority of the cooking or the majority of the cleaning, and
> it still falls into those kinds of, like, stereotypes, and I can't relate to

> that. I see it more as that we are all different as people and we all have
> strengths and weaknesses.

Yet there is an understanding that equality is very difficult to achieve.
Stephen demonstrates how it may be rendered even more difficult
where competition exists between partners with similar life goals:

> He was at a different stage of life from me. I was envisaging that I would
> build up my sort of life around my career and develop, and perhaps, you
> know, buy my first flat, and then suddenly I am thrown into this other
> world, where I don't have to worry about these things, but at the same
> time I don't have the sense of achievement that comes with all these
> things. So, it was a little bit awkward, for quite a bit of time.

Ted suggests how Michel Foucault's[3] understanding of equality as a
fluid concept has helped him understand the many changes in status
he has undergone in relationship:

> I like something that Michel Foucault wrote when he was about to die.
> He said that equality is not static. It means sometimes I'm in charge
> and sometimes you're in charge, and it flows back and forth very easily.
> It doesn't mean that at any one point we are exactly equal, no.

This realism about difference and the struggle to achieve equality-
in-relationship renders the research participants wary of merger or
enmeshment with each other, so that the theological ideas of becoming
in marriage one flesh, or of sacrificing self for the other as Christ
sacrificed himself for the Church, are critiqued. Christina explains, as
do others, that a vital quality of her partnership is remaining distinct,
enjoying difference, while fully embracing commitment to the other.
Self-sacrifice is understood in this way. The stress in the responses is

---

3   Michel Foucault (1926–1984) was a French philosopher, historian of
    ideas, social theorist and literary critic. He addressed the issue of equality
    in considering the relationship between power and knowledge, and how
    they are used as a form of social control through societal institutions. An
    introduction to his work, written by Lisa Downing, was published as a
    'Cambridge Introduction to Literature Paperback' in 2008.

on being able to freely and willingly give of the self on a daily basis, out of love for the other, rather than submerging need or character into the life of the other. Emma is particularly wary about the idea of self-sacrifice in relation to the history of women and marriage:

> The idea of sacrifice for the welfare of the other, mirroring the self-sacrifice of Christ for his church, I think is really problematic. Especially for women, I mean women in heterosexual relationships because of sexism. I think it's not just about sexism but maybe it is especially. One of the parts of the traditional Eucharist that always sticks in my throat a bit is 'Send us out in the power of the Spirit to be a living sacrifice'. And I know what they mean, but it's just so easy for women, especially, to take that too far, in my opinion. So, I am not very sacrificing! I am pretty good at getting my needs met, and I have to check that's not at the expense of my partner, that's she's not inadvertently sacrificing.

There is in the research participants' responses a loosening of pre-ordained shapes of relationships, particularly in the freedom of women to challenge patriarchal values in their closest relationships. Present too is the idea of entering a relationship for its own sake, expecting increasingly open communication, and the exposure of vulnerabilities. Certainly, there is a stress on equality in the emotional and practical processes of the relationship.

Yet there is also a clear and insistent emphasis on 'growing together in trust and love'. The most striking initial finding in conducting the interviews was the stress all participants placed on the intention to live together as partners for life. Ted describes this faithful commitment as an ascetical practice which creates trust and love:

> I think that in practising commitment to my partner, I gain the skill of being able to pay attention, make sacrifices when necessary, remember to be happy, all these things. So, through the doing, through the everyday living, and remembering to do it, that I'll achieve something that makes me happy ultimately and him too.

These thoughts of Ted return us to the idea of marriage as a gift of God as it is described by the queer theologian Eugene Rogers. For

Rogers marriage is 'an ascetic practice of and for the community by which God takes sexuality up and into God's triune life' (1999, p.73). Since we are created as bodies in the image of God, God finds ways to enter into communion with us through our bodies. By our focus on love for one person for life, and by the self-giving which takes place in that relationship, God uses bodies in marriage to be transformed into the image of Christ's self-giving love.

The delight and tenderness of sexual union

I asked very few questions about the role of sex in these relationships, inhibited perhaps by my priestly role with the participants, but perhaps also by my awareness as a former social worker and counsellor that in a one-to-one conversation of considerable length and intensity, held in a confined, private space for the sake of upholding confidentiality, to approach the topic of sex could be construed as intrusive, or inappropriately arousing, or both. As if confirming the wisdom of this approach, I noticed the playful, cheeky tone of conversation about sexual encounter in the pre-civil partnership stages of interviewees' lives. This playful content was lacking in the further discussion of their relationships of civil partnership. I was, after all, acquainted with, and might indeed interview, the partner. This was an area of life reserved for their conversation only.

Nevertheless, three aspects of these conversations deserve attention as they demonstrate participants challenging the Church of England's supposed norm of confining sexual activity to heterosexual marriage.

First, participants had sexual experience with other partners before entering this committed relationship. As discerned by Alan Wilson, so also for these participants, marriage has evolved away from the role of societal regulator of sexual behaviour towards that of 'relational gold standard' (2014, p.163). Sue had created her own ethics around sex, as had all participants, taken not from Anglican teaching about marriage but from popular culture, and from a sense of the importance of not doing harm in personal relationships:

> I couldn't understand how it could be all right, but surely it must be
> because you know, there were parameters – not sleeping around, not
> being destructive, the same as if I had been heterosexual, so in the
> context of a stable, loving monogamous relationship it must be all right.
> So, I sort of came to peace with it.

Rowan Williams in 'The Body's Grace' (1996) suggests that such encounters may themselves be 'graceful', a coming home in the body in the experience of another's desire, and may, as in the case of these participants, prompt longing for 'the fuller, longer exploration of the body's grace that faithfulness offers' (p.63).

Second, participants had no vocation to sexual celibacy within their civil partnerships, as the Church of England House of Bishops suggested ought to be the case for gay and lesbian Christians entering civil partnership to order their financial and legal affairs. Instead they understand their vows of commitment to assist them to remain sexually faithful. David is clear about this:

> Now, we are not saints! We remain faithful to each other and everything,
> but sometimes we don't behave well towards each other, but we have
> promised to do something in a way that we both believe in and those
> are the standards which we, um, when we calm down, and after a row
> or something like that, we remember and aspire to.

For Ted, it is the decision to enter a monogamous relationship that indicates a seriousness of intention:

> At that point where I had a tendency to sleep around deciding to be
> monogamous would be the marker of this is serious.

Echoing this change in sexual behaviour when a step of commitment is taken, Eugene Rogers in *Sexuality and the Christian Body* (1999) understands marriage to be a kind of ascetic practice, and argues that conservative protest against same-sex marriage denies same-sex couples 'true self-denial' (p.70).

Third, non-heterosexual sex and sex outside committed relationships are understood by participants as steps on the way to sexual fulfilment within the committed love represented by civil partnership and same-sex marriage. Ted suggests a further depth of meaning to committed sexual love, of risking openness to being known:

> It's the place that I end up showing as a person, that's not in a religious community, it's the place that I show the most of myself and try to work the hardest and letting the other person in on so many levels, including on the physical level, which is a whole thing that can't be separated from everything else, right, so, um, I don't say that like it's magical, but to me that's my sacramental theology.

Rowan Williams writes about the risky vulnerability involved in the 'spontaneous exposure' of sex in 'The Body's Grace' (1996): 'Sexual faithfulness is not an avoidance of risk, but the creation of a context in which grace can abound because there is a commitment not to run away from the perception of the other' (p.63).

The foundation of family life

I was struck by how often and positively participants mention creating a home, caring for relatives, and sharing household tasks. Sue talks of a home in which tasks are shared and time is enjoyed together:

> We just do logical splits – whoever is better at something because obviously we don't have the gender thing. I like doing the cooking and the shopping. So, I do it. My partner can do it, but she doesn't particularly enjoy it, so why suffer... My partner was at home for a few months because she was unemployed at one stage. That was great because she obviously took on all the house stuff. So, we had a great time, we had more time together, it worked quite well... I think we are our favourite people.

The couple also finds deliberate ways to balance the separate – togetherness continuum all relationships face:

> *We put in the diary times when we are going to go off and do other things and times when we are going to be together. We have 'keep frees' and 'outs'.*

Part of homemaking for these Christians is prayer, worship and Bible study within the home. Rogers writes that 'Christian marriage for lesbian and gay people…is a community, a little polity, a micrabasileia, a domestic church, a way of life under God' (1999, p.29). Anne speaks of placing prayer at the heart of her home with her partner:

> *We want to always make sure that we give time and space to God within the relationship. I mean, we always get a Lent Book and an Advent Book and we read it together on a daily basis, because that's something we want to do. There was a period of time when we couldn't find a church we wanted to go to, so we had our own services. And that wasn't something we just felt we ought to do, but something we really wanted to do… So, we are very faithful, I suppose, we want to include God in our life.*

Lucy, similarly, talks of pursuing Bible study in her family home, as her grandmother taught her to do:

> *My granny taught me to read by the Bible when I was very little, and my mum was unwell. So, it's kind of a comforting thing. But now in this partnership I feel secure enough to read more than the words. And what I normally tell people like my friend whose daughter I sometimes look after, and she says, 'How can you be a Christian if you're gay?' And I say it's more about the message than the words.*

Another part of home building is care for relatives, which takes all kinds of shapes and forms. David shares a country home not only with his partner but also with two old friends, their best friends, and their children. Lucy always wanted children and now has two. She suggests that both she and her partner, caught on camera or in a painting, would be looking at the children and not at each other. Anne talks movingly of being accepted into her partner's smaller family and is one of several research participants who value newfound warm support in a different family. Emma laughingly admits the cost of this care. She recalls the story of Ruth's loyalty to Naomi's family whenever she herself has no great desire to visit a demanding relative of her partner's family. Ted wryly admits that his partner seems more popular with some of his nieces and nephews than he is himself. Completely contrary to Giddens's predictions of modern relationships in *The Transformation of Intimacy* (1992), there is no severing of links with either children or intergenerational care in this group of research participants. One is a parent already; another looks forward to being so; two others share their home with a family that includes children; four regularly visit the children of friends and siblings. Four interviewees are closely involved in high levels of intergenerational care, while nine regularly visit parents or family, their own or those of their partner.

In addition to this sense of making home and welcoming family, there is a strong sense among the participants of being called to serve the community, whether that community is local, national or international, gay or straight, Christian or non-Christian. Emma speaks of the stability of her relationship helping to stretch her 'beyond herself and into the community', while David explains the over-spilling nature of love:

> *If you feel that the combination of the two of you in your love can be good not only to yourselves but also as an example to others and can somehow improve things for yourselves and others, then that is an example of doing what God has led you to do.*

What of homemaking for the purpose of the procreation of children? In 'Fecundity: Sex and Social Reproduction', Chapter 5 of *Queer Theology: Rethinking the Western Body*, David Matzko McCarthy (2007) rethinks the meaning of fruitfulness in intimate committed long-term relationships. He suggests that the social body may be mediated through sexual practices, not only by the procreation of children, but also by the creation of households in which there is space for committed belonging over time. This fruitfulness births three 'bodies' that give theological weight to the interviewees' love of home. First, it gives birth to a connected sexual and social life.

Instead of sex being considered at its best 'natural', 'wild', 'pre-social', 'nomadic' – ideas that lead ultimately to disloyalty being approved over stability – sex may be more appropriately subsumed by the character of household, creating bonds of family, home, hospitality. Second, sex that is about mutual belonging rather than the immediate gratification of desire gives birth to a belonging over time such that our presence cannot be exchanged for that of another. Our bodies are made by each other and known to each other as we learn to bear each other's presence in everyday life. So, we create what McCarthy calls 'the grammar of a shared life' (p.95) – sleeping in the same bed, breaking bread, offering our bodily presence in sickness and health. Third, such fruitfulness gives birth to sex as passionate play, honouring the lifecycle and its rhythms, instead of being valued for the rekindling of youthful inexhaustible desire.

McCarthy (2007) suggests that same-sex unions may produce three fruits, which are demonstrated in the narratives of these research participants. They may be procreative precisely by creating home, being present sexually to each other over time, repeating everyday activities in a shared space. They may shape the social self and the social world in imitation of Christ. They may bear the fruit of ordinary self-giving to the other and to the world.

Made holy by God

In exploring biblical imagery for the meaning of their civil partnership, five participants use the word *covenant* to express something of the relationship's dependency on God's activity. Emma likens her relationship to a three-legged stool:

> *...when we married in 1995, we viewed the marriage as a three-way relationship, between us and God...without God this three-legged stool would fall over.*

David explores what this covenantal aspect means for him and his partner:

> For me, the ceremony and the vows we made in church had the nature
> of a covenant because they were promises, and as Christians they were
> even more significant than that because they weren't just promises
> between me and my partner but there was certainly a three-way
> contract between me, my partner and God, witnessed importantly by
> our family and friends and supporters. And it was important that the
> ceremony was conducted by a minister of the Church.

For theologians exploring the theological meanings in same-sex relationships, the theme of marriage as a covenant with God has been a rich seam to mine. Pertinent to research participants' understanding of their relationships as being reflective of God's covenant love with his people is Robert Song's focus in *Covenant Calling: Towards a Theology of Same-Sex Relationships* (2014) on faithfulness, mutuality and fruitfulness as signs of that reflection, and his sense of human relationships looking for future consummation in the Resurrection. There is a strong sense of this moving towards a final consummation in Sue's interpretation of her relationship of 'becoming more Christ-like', and in Matthew's of 'becoming transformed in the direction of self-giving'.

Sue's and Matthew's interpretations of living in a covenant relationship with God are also resonant with the language of Jensen in 'God's desire for us: Reformed theology and the question of same-sex marriage' (2006). For Jensen, marriage is a covenant, a partnership, an intimation of God's relationship with God's people, given as a gift from God for the well-being of the couple and the community. The desire for marriage is not merely desire for sex but for the whole person with whom one journeys under the mystery of God's grace for life. In the reform tradition, all human relating is understood to be broken, and God's grace a gift to which we respond feebly as we confess our need for communion with God and with each other. In this tradition, the married couple is always on a journey towards Christian marriage in a covenant pledged for a lifetime before God and the community of faith. What authorizes a Christian marriage are the promises of God, echoed in the promises of the couple and the community of faith. 'The witness of same sex couples in the Church, the Body of Christ, may suggest that these couples already live under the law of marriage, even when ecclesial practice and societal law refuse them access to marriage' (Jensen 2006, p.18).

Matthew's understanding of what happened at his civil partnership and at the religious celebration of that partnership is resonant with this understanding:

> *Being in a civil partnership means that in addition to being committed to the other person, to my partner, I also keep questioning of self, what is the place of ourselves as a couple in our community?... I think that in the Holy Spirit we were lifted...and supported...with that strength we have more capacity to think about our position for the community.*

Matthew's interview is rich in a spiritual understanding of his relationship. He seems, to his own surprise, to indeed live under the law of marriage as Jensen suggests same-sex couples may. He struggles, since English is not his first language, to articulate the truth that he perceives himself to be doing the prophetic work of God in same-sex marriage, even while being in a civil partnership. In terms of God's prophetic activity in human lives, he considers himself to be already married:

> *Well, we want this marriage. That's the goal. But the civil partnership... I treat it in the same way, at least in relation to our development... So, in relation to our growth, it's not like I am not married, not involved in this prophetic work.*

If covenant means promise of faithfulness, presence, journey and interaction with God, it also means for Stephen living under the protective canopy of God. He describes the rite of religious celebration of his civil partnership, which he calls a wedding, like this:

> *It was almost like the social and the spiritual world coming together, in this one moment.*

Here there is a mystical understanding of covenant love that resembles that of Rogers in his writing about same-sex marriage. Since we are created as bodies in the image of God, God finds ways to enter into communion with us through our bodies. By our focus on love for one person for life, and by the self-giving that takes place in that relationship, God uses bodies in marriage to be transformed into the image of Christ's desire for us his Church, and of his self-giving to us through the offering of his body. The communion that flows from God to interpenetrate the couple in marriage is one demonstration of God's desire for us (Rogers 1999).

Conclusion: Is this marriage or not?

Yes, it is marriage. The defining marks of such marriage are these:

- The intention to love and care for the other for life, and to be open to the possibility of being loved and known by the other for life. This intention rests on the possibility of growing in forgiveness and trust towards the other, of growing more Christ-like in that love.
- The promise to maintain faithfulness, to strive for equality, to enjoy the differences within the relationship, and to struggle for transformation in the direction of self-giving.
- The vow to create a household in which tasks are shared, sex is enjoyed as non-competitive play, which is creative of lifelong relationship in which the beloved other is known as irreplaceable, space is created for togetherness and apartness, and into which family and friends are welcomed.
- The hope to use the energy created by such stability to serve the community.
- The understanding that God as Trinity has been present in whatever suffering the partners may have endured, or whatever suffering they may yet endure, to rescue and to be alongside.
- The faith that God as Son is present wherever the couple's table feasts are stretched to include the stranger who may be alone and in need as they were once.
- The trust that God the Spirit will bring all things to a completion of God's love, which both is present and is to come.

Althaus-Reid (2008) complained that in the rush to gain equality of opportunity between women and men in the Church, feminist theology lost the capacity to continue to sharpen a feminist deconstruction of heteropatriarchy in theology and Church. As a woman who became a priest in the first wave of Church of England ordinations in 1994, I understand this criticism. Feminist theology, after enjoying a burst of creativity for 20 years around the fringes of the Church of England before those ordinations, has been safely sidelined in the Church's liturgy, preaching and teaching, as the Church has engaged in the struggle for women to become bishops.

However, the rush towards equality for gay and lesbian people to be married may have a more lasting effect, since our presence in the institution of marriage queers marriage in highly visible ways. It queers the language of marriage, since gay and lesbian partners cannot be husband and wife. It queers assumed gender roles and power differentiations, since within a same-sex relationship these roles, as we have seen, are determined by other means. It queers the meaning and the means of procreation, whether children are born to the marriage or not. It queers heteronormative assumptions about sex, and its potential role in the growth towards holiness. It queers the meaning and place of God's blessing. As Emma exulted:

> I think that by being in a marriage we are subverting heterosexual norms within society. And I love that! You know I have had many discussions with feminist lesbian friends about marriage and patriarchy. Why they may want to be in a civil partnership rather than a marriage because of what queer means. But I think there is nothing queerer than two women or two men being in a marriage. It's fantastic.

These relationships are sacramental in showing meanings of God's presence. They demonstrate engagement with the liberating language and activity of God. For me, despite my earlier resistance, it is inescapably evident that the relationships we have learnt about on this journey represent marriage. However, many Christians disagree, and it is to their serious concerns that I now turn.

Chapter 6

PAUSE FOR THOUGHT

Conflicting Views and Opposing Arguments

> *There's a slight niggle at the back of my mind. What if I am wrong?*
>
> Sue (research participant)

The journey so far

In this book I have explored the language that 13 gay and lesbian Christians, who are in civil partnerships, use to describe their relationships of long-term commitment and intimacy. I have suggested that these relationships participate in sacramental reality, that they reflect the liberating activity of God in the world, and that theologically and relationally they constitute marriage. I have reflected how queer theology may act as a lens through which to ask the question of how heteronormative theology supports the relationships of heterosexual people while diminishing the worth of gay and lesbian relationships. The use of this lens has encouraged me to discern God's presence in so-called 'outsider' people and places, to find God acting and speaking outside the boundaries of heterosexual relationships, and to celebrate the blessing of God in same-sex marriage. I have discovered a queer God, not in the sense of knowing or defining God's being, for that would be blasphemy, but in the sense of understanding how queer language about God may enlarge our vision of the people, places and relationships in which the revelation of God occurs.

However, far from there being agreement about these views, the subject of homosexuality, Christianity and same-sex marriage is the cause of vigorous, sometimes fierce, ongoing debate within Christian families and communities, and within and between Christian denominations. Anne, a participant in this study, belongs to a family in which many members belong to the Church of England. She senses that her relationship is not considered in as serious a light as marriage would be, and that an open family celebration of her own family with her partner's family would prove impossible. She dearly longs for marriage in church, but meanwhile felt obliged to register her civil partnership in a quiet, unobtrusive way:

> My partner's mother and my father have a very strong faith, and a very different faith, and there are a lot of religious connections in my family anyway. I would have been worried that something was going to happen, so we thought, if you cannot invite everybody, we cannot invite anybody.

A poignant part of Anne's testimony is that, so strong is the Christian faith at the heart of her relationship with her partner, knowing as they did that a civic ceremony cannot include religious content, they nevertheless registered their protest about this at the register office and call their registration a 'service':

> The service was lovely. We had written the service, and we had, we were very clear that we would have liked some religious ceremony in it if we could, but obviously we weren't allowed to do it in civic ceremonies. We wanted to make sure that we acknowledged that fact.

Christina belongs to a Roman Catholic family. Despite the liberal flavour of that family's faith, she felt that she lived without complete self-acceptance until the public celebration of her relationship of civil partnership among family and friends:

> *Homosexuality was utterly taboo, in the sense at any rate of being*
> *rendered utterly invisible and unacceptable, and not to be acknowledged*
> *or talked about. Taboo has notions of...being unclean and defiling, and*
> *that was implicit in the culture I grew up in, and sinful.*

What are the reasons given for such disagreement among Christians? Those who argue against same-sex marriage being celebrated in state and Church contest that it is contrary to God's will as revealed in the Bible, and that it ignores the authority of centuries of Church tradition. In this chapter I suggest that the Christians I interviewed ignored none of these sources of theological insight. On the contrary, they demonstrate wrestling with their interpretation of those sources, often painfully, respectfully, and for many years. It is their experience of committed faithful loving and of being loved, and of doing this in the context of faith, worship, prayer, Bible study and Church belonging, that persuades them that God is doing a new thing in their lives.

The authority of Scripture

The Bible is the record of a past culture that, even as a classic spiritual text, deserves the engagement of non-believers as a collection of accounts of who human beings are and what it may mean to live well. But to Christians it is a sacred text, a witness to God's involvement in the world, and a locus of God's self-revelation. At the very centre of Christian life is Jesus of Nazareth, whom Christians believe to be God's self-utterance, the Word of God made flesh in human history. Because the Hebrew Scriptures, the 'Old Testament', were the Scriptures that Jesus used, and the Christian Scriptures, the 'New Testament', the earliest reflection on the meaning of his life, death and resurrection for the world, the Bible is 'the primary and critical link of all subsequent generations to Jesus Christ' (Volf 2010, p.6). Therefore, Christians search the Scriptures asking not only what does this text mean, but also how is God addressing them? Christians read the Scriptures with the expectation that God will show them what it is to belong to the Kingdom of God now.

So, the testimony of the Christians interviewed for this study is that they read the Bible as people of faith, seeking God's will for their lives. Lucy describes evenings where with her small child and partner present in her home,

> I'll sit here with my Bible study books and that's just how we are.

Anne is clear that her partner Sue brought her back to Church after a long absence. She has helped her understand her faith 'because she knows far more about faith, religion, Church history, the Bible' so that now they pray together and study together through Lent and Advent. She states:

> We bring God into our relationship...we want to always make sure that we give time and space to God within the relationship.

She describes a living faith in which Jesus is present encouraging them:

> ...he would say what a good relationship you two have got and encourage it and that does strengthen me.

David, reflecting on a sermon based on stories in the books of Ezra and Nehemiah, in which Jews returning from exile in Babylon to rebuild the city of Jerusalem are called 'repairers of the breach', demonstrates, as we saw in Chapter 3, the way in which lesbian and gay Christians may respect, recite and receive the Word of God for them personally, with implications for ethics, in the context of Church:

> I do think that the return from exile story is one which metaphorically matters, because it was the story of both what was offered to those returning, the promise of freedom in God, but also the responsibility that they held to make the most of what was given to them through that return from exile. They became the 'repairers of the breach'.
>
> That's an important message...I think, because we must make what we can of what we've got, we must not hide our light under a bushel basket. And I think that if you feel drawn to somebody in love, and you feel that that combination of the two of you in your love can be

good, not only to yourselves but also as an example to others, and can
somehow improve things for yourselves and others, then that is an
example of doing what God has led you to do.

This interpretation of the story of exile reminds us that a queer reading of the Bible may be simply understood as a reading done by queer readers, who search, wrestle with and examine the Bible for its meaning for them in the context of the body of all believers. However, in doing this, they stumble over a tension that exists for all Christians in reading the Scriptures, which acts as a source of much disagreement over the theological meaning of lesbian and gay relationships. In reading the Bible, all Christians expect to be spoken to by God, to be people to whom God is revealed and God's promises given. Yet the Bible is also a collection of very different sorts of material, the historical nature of which creates a huge diversity of voice and perspective. Miroslav Volf helpfully describes this diversity of voices:

The Bible is about God speaking and acting in given times and spaces, addressing people living in distinct cultures, shaped by individual histories and the specific convergence of influences, beset by diverse concrete problems, and carried on the wings of many distinct hopes. (2010, p.24)

Understanding this diversity of voice a tension emerges. How do we both honour the overarching story of the Bible – a testimony to God's love revealed for all people in creation, covenant, salvation through Christ, the building of the community of Church and the future hope of heaven – and yet respect the concrete character of its very diverse and specific texts? Volf admits the difficulty: 'To respect the integrity of both at the same time is difficult' (p.25). Lucy, an interviewee, has begun to feel free to live this tension, which she expresses as a matter of Church belonging:

I am so secure in my relationship that I feel less and less bothered what
other people think. I feel freer to explore my faith from the very Baptist
and evangelical church way that I was brought up to read the Bible,

> *combined with St Martin-in-the-Fields to dip my head in and twist my*
> *head around every single Sunday!*

Wrestling with the tension of Biblical interpretation

Lesbian and gay Christians, and their supporters, who wish neither to discard the Bible nor to discount the existence of a transcendent God who confronts the world in the name of justice and holiness, face difficulty. For there are texts in the Old and New Testaments that, in their historical specificity, appear to condemn homosexual and lesbian relationships. The texts are these: Genesis 19:1–8 and 24–25; Leviticus 18:22 and 20:13; 1 Corinthians 6:9–10; 1 Timothy 1:9–10; Romans 1:18–32. What did these texts mean, perhaps, in their own context, and what may they mean for us?

Genesis 19:1–8, 24–25

In the book of Genesis, guests, who are messengers from God in disguise, have arrived at Lot's house. Lot is anxious to offer them hospitality. However, townsmen of Sodom bang on the door wanting to commit sexual acts with these strangers. Lot is so intent on their care that he offers instead his daughters to the men of Sodom. God is so enraged with the behaviour of the townsmen that he destroys both Sodom and Gomorrah in a vast volcanic eruption.

The message of the text, given the willingness of Lot to allow his daughters to be raped, is unlikely to have concerned sexual ethics. It appears to concern instead the importance of showing hospitality to strangers, who may be messengers of God. Wrestling with the text, and offering a queer critique of interpretations that condemn homosexuality in its light, we may question why homosexuality is focused on as the apparent sin deserving of divine judgement here. An alternative reading of the text may result in our questioning our own attitude towards strangers who ask for our help, and the lengths to which we are willing to go to provide them with hospitality.

Leviticus 18:22, 20:13

The texts in the book of Leviticus appear to more clearly condemn the anal penetration of one man by another. Examining their context, however, we notice that they are part of the 'Holiness Codes'. These codes were compiled over three centuries of history and were intended to help maintain the purity of the Jews when they were held captive in Babylon. To remain distinct from their surrounding communities, activities that depended upon the total separation of objects and people – of foods, of fibres, of vegetable and plant seeds, of men and women – were insisted upon by the code writers. A strict order of things, including the roles of men and women, underlie many of the prohibitions. For men to take the subordinate role of women in sexual activity is prohibited, as is the waste of 'seed'.

In interpreting these texts for today a queer biblical scholar may ask why sexual activity between men is singled out for obedience from among those many other prohibitions contained in the Holiness Codes that we ignore completely. Again, in the cultures for which the Holiness Codes were written, the sexual role of women in heterosexual intercourse was deemed inferior to that of men, so that men accepting the seemingly more passive receptive role of women in intercourse were deemed to have lost that which distinguished them as male. Thoughtful reflection around these texts may result in our realizing that we no longer differentiate in precisely this way between the roles of women and men in sexual activity, so that the rationale for the condemnation of anal sex is lost.

1 Corinthians 6:9-10 and 1 Timothy 1:9-10

In both 1 Corinthians and 1 Timothy, Paul uses the Greek words *malakoi* for 'male prostitutes', and *arsenokoites* for 'sodomites'. Both terms are likely to have described exploitative relationships with male slaves or dependents, and to have been condemned by Paul either because he considered them abusive or to be pagan phenomena. Thoughtful consideration of these texts may, however, persuade us to consider our own use of power in relationship, rather than to equate these terms with the condemnation of homosexual relationships of longevity, equality and loving commitment.

Romans 1:18-32

In Romans 1:18–32 Paul links homosexual practice in both men and women with idolatry. In the context of pagan idol worship, men and women were condemned by Paul for engaging in same-sex activity with each other and with cult prostitutes. What was for Paul the worship of God, and the regard for the natural and hierarchical ordering of male and female relationships, were lost in such practices.

Struggling to understand these lines, Oliver O'Donovan, in *A Conversation Waiting to Begin* (2009), urges us not to rule out inconvenient angles in this text (p.67). He offers us an example of wrestling with what it may mean to bring to such a text thoughtful obedience and respect, by recognizing that we too may need in our culture and time to bring our own sexual idolatries under scrutiny. We in our own time may need to ask what Christian freedom means in the context of our own culture, and what are the idolatrous practices to which we are likely to succumb?

These texts may leave us feeling upset or bewildered. In such upset and puzzlement, it is helpful to consider the difference between implicit obedience to the content of the texts and utter disregard of their meaning, and to reject both as a way forward to understanding. In obedience to the apparent literal truth of the texts, we lose sight of the distance that necessarily exists between the cultures for which those texts were written and our own understanding of language, motivation and human relationships. This gap in understanding is not easily filled. How we now understand the words of the text can never be precisely the same as the meaning of the texts to their original authors and hearers. Nor can we discern everything of God's mind concerning the subject of this text, for the mind of God is always waiting to be revealed. A thoughtful reflection that continues to experience humility and confusion, and is unafraid to admit both, is a path forwards in understanding. Sue, again as we read in Chapter 3, recognizes the experience of such bewilderment and confusion:

> *I remember going for a walk and having one of those conversations with God which you occasionally have to have. I was talking out loud and saying, 'Look, the thing is, the situation appears to be, God, in case you hadn't noticed, this appears to be happening on the sexuality front.' There was a one-way conversation and I said, 'It follows that you must have made me like this. You have either made a mess of this, which I*

> can't believe, or it's true, this is the situation. So, the only other option
> is you made me, and I happen to be a lesbian so...' So, I came to be at
> peace with myself about it I suppose.
>   I have had the wobbles since. There's a slight niggle at the back of
> my mind. What if I am wrong? And God's really annoyed?

After this Sue searches the Scriptures for signs that a relationship springs from, and is rooted in, faith in God. She finds such signs in the New Testament and accepts that she sees the fruits of the Holy Spirit burgeoning in her own partnership:

> So now I suppose that I am in a position where I think that something
> so good and something so pure – pure is not quite the right word, but
> sort of, good and honest and truthful and faithful – can't be wrong
> but must have something 'God-ish' about it. Or perhaps better Christ-
> like. It sounds a bit pretentious but you know a snapshot of the Divine,
> you know that whole thing about honesty and truth and openness and
> kindness and love, you know things in Corinthians about what love is,
> they are all pictures of God, aren't they?

Sue's faith, rooted in Scripture, she finds effective. She finds herself growing in a Christ-like way:

> It [the partnership] brings out the best in me. I am probably at my best
> when I am loved... So I am more like Christ although still a long way
> off. [laughs] I mean that I am heading in the right direction. You want
> to be the best that you are for the person that you love.

Biblical texts that concern the right ordering of human relationships, or the idolatrous cultures on which we become fixated, or hospitality to strangers, or holiness of life, continue to invite us to struggle with their meaning. We interrogate such texts, and expect them to interrogate us, concerning the meanings of God for our lives. One lens through which to interrogate them is a queer lens. This queer lens prompts us to remember that the Bible has a long history of misuse. Its texts may be used as weapons by the powerful against the weak, and indeed by victims against their oppressors, thus merely turning the tables of powerful revulsion and hate in the opposite direction. We are less likely to misuse the Bible if we ask of our interpretations: who is excluded here? Why, and how may they be included?

Queer inclusion in the Bible

Susannah Cornwall in *Controversies in Queer Theology* (2011, pp.114–143) offers, in addition to the Bible being read queerly because a queer reader is reading it, four ways of including queer experience in the content and reach of the Bible. Queer 'traces' may be found offering queer encouragement. In the book of Ruth, the eponymous character declares to Naomi that 'Your people shall be my people and your God my God' (Ruth 1:16). This single text proved the text most used by the participants in this study in their civil partnership rites and celebrations. One participant, Anne, interpreted it quite unselfconsciously in a queer way:

> ...you know the whole thing about that feels to me like the inclusion of being part of a community of lesbians, if you like. The 'your people shall be my people' is really important to me in the sense that I get a lot of strength from being with other couples who are lesbians too, because we just relax and be ourselves. It's never quite that way with straight couples.

Another queer 'trace' is found by Hanks (1997, p.139, pp.142–144) in Paul, who greets a large number of unusual households not headed by a married man in the Epistle to the Romans. Similarly, Eugene F. Rogers (2009, pp.19–33) uses the word *queer* to mean the querying of the meaning of social roles in Paul's understanding of how 'in Christ, there is no longer Jew or Greek, there is no longer slave nor free, there is no longer male nor female' (Galatians 3:27–28).

Other queer writers find queer ancestors in the text, such as the much-praised 'eunuchs' in the New Testament, whom Kolakowski (1997, p.47) identifies as the forebears of transgender people. In the same way, Nancy Wilson (1995, pp.148–164) celebrates Lydia, the business-woman and head of a household in Acts 16, and the centurion with deep affection for his ill servant in Matthew 8 and Luke 7.

Still other scholars read the Bible in a queer way by adopting methods to subvert its traditional meanings. So, Koch (2006) asks what we find when, instead of making ourselves the 'man of unclean lips' in Isaiah 6:5–8, we read ourselves into the position of being the seraph bearing a burning coal? 'This is the seraphic task of those of us engaged with biblical studies on the behalf of the LGBT community: to choose the right coal for the right situation' (p.355). Koch uses this as a strategy of empowerment for disempowered readers and worshippers.

However, I find these methods of including queer experience in the reading of the Bible risky, and ultimately unsatisfying, in that they allow queer interpretation to remain what Cornwall (2011, pp.127–128) describes as a 'ghettoized interest', and restrict queer concerns only to queer people. To read the Bible in this way appears to mimic its privileged reading in a conservative way by heterosexual people, and to risk losing its transcendent meaning and challenge. Far more satisfying and far-reaching in its implications is the search for overarching themes within the Bible. When we discover such themes, we notice, on the one hand, how applicable they may be to the lives of gay and lesbian Christians. On the other hand, we may discern how their expression in heteronormative ways may be challenged by the experiences and faith journeys of gay and lesbian Christians.

One such interpretative method is suggested by Samuel Wells in *How Then Shall We Live?* (2016, pp.99–115). In a chapter concerning LGBT identity, Wells asks how lesbian and gay people may be considered as a gift and blessing to the Church, rather than a burden, a 'problem to be solved'. He attempts to change the terms of the debate so that we concentrate not on individual texts but on the whole story that we join when we become Christian. The story of Creation, Covenant, Christ, Church and Consummation he stands on its head. Rather than beginning with 'how we were made', he asks 'for what we were made', and therefore what kind of living will reflect the breathtaking destiny of us all in the consummation of God's time. He understands LGBT people to be different from, but not less than, heterosexual people, and called in the same way to display the fruits of the Holy Spirit in the ways we integrate our sexuality with our Christian discipleship. Perhaps most encouragingly in terms of an

inclusive reading of the Bible, Wells suggests that we are all called to
bear in our bodies the truth of God sharing our life in the incarnate
Christ, the goodness of Christ's laying down his life for our sake, and
the beauty of the Holy Spirit's raising Christ to life for evermore. The
Church needs everyone to do this, not least those LGBT people who
have already been persecuted for their faith, yet who remain faithful
Christians. The dynamic energy of this writing is reflected in David's
understanding that he is created in God's image:

> I get more and more out of the Bible as I get older and as I learn to read
> it. It, and what I read there, is part of everything... We are all created in
> the image of God. And essentially because I know what is good within
> me, and what is not, I have never had a moral or religious problem
> with my sexuality.

It is reflected in Vanessa's 'coming home' to her Christian identity:

> Opening up that door again to God, it was refreshing because I allowed
> myself to be fully loved by God, every aspect of myself, and also loving
> back.

And it is reflected in Matthew's animation by the Holy Spirit in the
service of Holy Communion giving thanks for his civil partnership:

> I think that in the Holy Spirit we were lifted... We receive the additional
> strength of being supported, but with that strength we have the capacity
> to think about our position in the community.

Church tradition

The Church of England, which was the context for my research,
understands itself to be both 'catholic and reformed'. Since the
Reformation, which brought it into being, the Church of England's
formal statements have therefore revealed reverence for the authority
of both Scripture and Church tradition. In its recent statements
concerning same-sex marriage (Church of England 2014), marriage
between a man and a woman is to be understood as a 'creation

ordinance', showing God's gift and grace, and to be central to the stability and health of human society, providing the only permitted context for sexual intercourse and the best possible context for the raising of children. The Church of England offers no authorized acts of worship to follow either civil partnership registration or civil same-sex marriage. Church of England clergy who are gay and lesbian are forbidden marriage. Should they enter civil partnerships, the understanding is that they should maintain the discipline of celibacy.

It is possible to see in the statements of the Church of England the influence of both conservative biblical interpretation and the belief in natural law outlined in the Catechism of the Catholic Church.[1] This Catechism, although not fully representing the full range of contemporary catholic thinking, gives expression to the traditional position of the Church when it states:

> Basing itself on Sacred Scripture, which presents homosexual acts as acts of grave depravity, Tradition has always declared that 'homosexual acts are intrinsically disordered'. They are contrary to the natural law. They close the sexual act to the gift of life. They do not proceed from a genuine and sexual complementarity. Under no circumstances can they be approved. (pp.504–505)

The Catechism of the Roman Catholic Church moves on to state that marriage between a man and a woman reflects God's design in creation. Genesis 1 and the Sixth Commandment are understood to signify a call to full sexual integration by accepting our sexual identity as male and female. Our human sexual identity is understood in the Catechism to reach its full expression in relationships of gender complementarity. Sex is understood to be given by God for pleasure in marriage and particularly to reach its purpose in the procreation of children. Neither homosexual acts, nor the relationships containing them, are to be approved since they are contrary to this natural law, are not procreative, and possess neither affective nor sexual complementarity. Natural law, the understanding that the moral standards that govern human behaviour are, in some sense,

1   www.vatican.va/archive/ccc_css/archive/catechism/p3s2c2a6.htm#2357

objectively derived from the nature of human beings and the nature of the world, and the wisdom of the Scriptures are not understood as expressions of culture, but as divine revelation discernible by reason. This is clearly expressed in the Second Vatican Ecumenical Council report, *Gaudium et Spes*:

> All evolution of morals and every type of life must be kept within the limits imposed by the immutable principles based upon every human person's constitutive elements and essential relations – these elements and relations transcend historical contingency. (Pastoral Constitution on the Church and the Modern World 1965, p.1037)

So, the English text of the report of the Roman Catholic Synod on the Family, which was published on 30 October 2014, contained the words: 'There are absolutely no grounds for considering homosexual unions to be in any way similar to or even remotely analogous to God's plan for marriage and the family' (Vatican Report of the Synod on the Family 2014).

The argument that gender and sexuality may be so strictly categorized, however, has been subject to social and scientific critique. In 1948 in the United States, Kinsey, Pomeroy and Martin published *Sexual Behavior in the Human Male*. They had developed the Heterosexual–Homosexual Rating Scale, commonly known as the Kinsey Scale, to account for research findings that showed people did not fit into exclusive heterosexual or homosexual categories. In their surveys, 37 per cent of men had homosexual experience, while only 4 per cent responded that they had been homosexual for their entire life. This report, together with a further report published in 1953 about female sexual behaviour, is associated with a change in public perception of sexuality. The publication of over 200 scales since then supports a far greater range of description. In 2008, Lisa Diamond, Professor of Developmental Psychology and Health Psychology at the University of Utah, published the results of a ten-year longitudinal study of 100 non-heterosexual women (Diamond 2008). Women in her study reported variability in their sexual orientation. Diamond concluded not that sexual orientation is chosen but that it may shift non-voluntarily for some women.

Alan Wilson is an Anglican Bishop who, like other recent Anglican authors (e.g. Ford 2019; Thatcher 2011), is persuaded by late 20th-century research in biology and the social sciences to suggest that the sexual dimension of being human may be understood as diverse, ambiguous and deeply personal rather than as simply binary (Wilson 2014, pp.163–164). He argues that at least four elements – biological sex; sexual orientation; gender identity; gender expression – themselves varied and multi-layered in texture, are joined in our sexual identity. To be homosexual or lesbian is therefore to be but one variation among very many others. Ford summarizes in her work *God, Gender, Sex and Marriage* (2019, pp.56–57) the reasons for which scientists now recognize three different factors that influence gender. The factors she explores are biology, gender identification and gender expression. She demonstrates how biological sex exists on a spectrum, how gender self-identification may in rare cases be different from that of a person's biological sex, and how in terms of gender expression attributes labelled masculine or feminine vary between cultures.

Given our changing understandings of gender and sexual orientation to include more fluid descriptions of both, how may queer Christians, their families and friends, mine Church tradition for rich seams of wisdom?

There are three paths to explore in relation to exploiting rather than discarding Church tradition from a queer point of view. The first is to honour the experience of gay and lesbian Christians and to understand experience as vital in the renewal of Christian theology and faith. The second is to ask: what is the 'usable past' in the Christian tradition? The third is to ask how queer experience may enrich the meaning of Christian marriage.

The use of experience

In this book, experience is understood as the contemporary living of relationships and events, together with the emotions, sensations, insights and understandings that accompany this lived reality. In this sense, the experience of gay and lesbian people is used to illustrate or develop an argument. Such experience, however, is not intended to represent an incontestable seam of insight. The Christians involved in this study at no point intended to suggest that 'anything goes' in their wrestling with sexual ethics and theology. Nor did they fall back on their experience as a final arbiter in decision making. On the contrary, the strength of their testimony lies in their demonstration that the meanings they ascribe to their relationships should in their view cohere with their whole understanding of what it is to be Christian. Their experience is for them a necessary source of theological insight, but it is not of itself a sufficient source.

In what sense, then, is experience authoritative in the interpretation of Christian tradition? It is authoritative in two ways. First, it provides useful stimulus to correct the assumption that living Christian tradition is simply that which has been always thought and practised. Joseph Ratzinger, later Pope Benedict XVI, suggests how important it is to question this assumption:

> Not everything that exists in the Church must for that reason be always a legitimate tradition; in other words, not every tradition that arises in the Church is a true celebration and keeping present of the mystery of Christ. There is a distorting, as well as legitimate tradition… Consequently, tradition must not be considered only affirmatively, but also critically. (1969, p.185)

Second, experience is authoritative in creating the circumstances in which believers recognize truths offered by the tradition. The moral authority of any source of theology is ultimately dependent on individuals' resonance with and recognition of the truth it offers. Experience brings Christian tradition alive, so that the rationales behind long-standing beliefs must remain persuasive. They must 'ring true' in terms of both the tradition as a whole and the life and experience of enquirers and believers. Sometimes new and better rationales must be found to undergird ongoing beliefs, or beliefs themselves may evolve in their meaning and sometimes even be replaced. So, clearly, former understandings of Church tradition have been challenged and replaced in the past in regard to slavery, to race equality, to usury and to the status and rights of women.

It is in the context of this understanding of the roles played by contemporary experience in bringing Christian tradition to life that I judge three areas of human experience are neglected in the arguments of those who oppose the blessing of same-sex love. First, pain of body and spirit forces us to think in new ways about sexual orientation and gender roles. What was assumed to be based in nature, in the given-ness of anatomy and physiology, and what was unquestioned, considered benign, in gendered divisions of labour, has been challenged by feminists, womanists, and gay and lesbian people suffering a painful lack of self-determining freedom to grow, to exert influence, even to protect the self from violence. Second, just as every secular discipline requires careful examination and interpretation, so do texts of the Bible and the writings of Church tradition. The cultures represented in the Bible and the traditions of the Church were neither stable nor monolithic. Third, at the heart of Christianity lies the awareness of God's justice and God's love, revealed in the person, words and work of Jesus. Since Jesus's summary of the religious tradition which he inherited stressed love of God, love of self, and love of neighbour, God's righteousness appears to call us to an inward wholeness of love, which extends to neighbours near and far. This orientation towards God involves the recognition that our judgements have the capacity for harm as well as healing of our neighbour, and that in the creation of theology and sexual ethics it is important not to neglect justice.

Finding the usable past

In Margaret Farley's work *Just Love: A Framework for Christian Sexual Ethics* (2010, pp.185–186), she accepts the challenge both to absorb Christian tradition as a source of theology and to offer a critique based on the authority of experience as another source. Accepting that cultural and social forces shaped our sexual desires, and therefore writings about those desires, Farley asks, What is the 'usable past' (p.187) in the Christian tradition? By this she does not mean cherry-picking our way around Christian tradition to support facile thoughts and arguments, but instead the rigorous task that honours all sources of theology and sets them in serious dialogue with each other:

> How to excavate historical layers of meaning, find lost treasures, take account of historical and cultural contexts for church life, hold on to gems of revelatory experience and shared faith: this is the question for those who go to tradition as a source of contemporary moral and theological insight. (p.187)

Searching Church tradition for ways forward in sexual ethics that recognize recent cultural shifts in the understanding of personal relationships, gender and sexual orientation, Farley suggests that we move away from a framework for sexual ethics based on the fear of taboo, an ethics of defilement and guilt, and towards an ethic for both heterosexual and homosexual relationships based on justice. Christina developed this theme of just action in the gradual eroding of taboo in her interview:

> *I thought that it was not only a joy but also a responsibility to have a civil partnership when it became available, and I feel rather the same about the marriage question. I feel that we have been hidden, silenced, taboo, rendered unacceptable and invisible, and that therefore it is prophetic to celebrate the love we have, and that we can experience it as God-given, and to make that visible. That provides a source of encouragement to others – taboo overcome a little.*

Farley (2010) finds rich strands within Christian tradition that support the autonomy and relationality of persons, which underline the importance of truth telling, which respect mutuality, equality and commitment, which encourage fruitfulness, and which recognize the demands of social justice. From the position of one mining the rich store of this usable past she encourages the Church to consider its own role in creating conditions for the respect of gay and lesbian persons, for truth telling about relationships, for offering rites and support systems to honour partners making lifelong commitments to each other, to recognize diverse forms of fruitfulness, and above all to examine its own role in supporting or undermining social justice for gay and lesbian people. She uses the Christian tradition in relation to social justice to challenge the Church's own interpretation of that tradition. She finds the usable past to offer a path of renewal:

The Christian community, in particular, is faced with serious questions… If, for example, a norm of commitment is appropriate for sexual relationships among Christians, and if such a norm belongs to a same sex ethic as much as to a heterosexual ethic, then the problems of institutional support must be addressed anew. (p.291)

Using the lens of queer experience

In this book I have explored the ways in which my interviewees interpret their relationships in the light of the theology of marriage. I suggest that by inhabiting the theology of marriage as same-sex couples, they 'queer' the meanings of marriage in highly visible ways. For example, the very language of marriage is queered since gay and lesbian partners cannot be husband and wife. Furthermore, gender roles and power differentiations are queered since in a same-sex partnership they must be determined in new, non-assumed ways. Finally, they also queer the meaning and means of procreation, and heteronormative assumptions about sex. Here, I want to suggest a way in which queer theology may throw new light on the meaning of God's blessing of their relationships. I do this to demonstrate one example of how the use of queer theology as a conceptual tool can help create an enriched theology of relationships.

In 'The Relationship of Bodies', the queer theologian David Matzo McCarthy (2002, pp.200–216) asks how the intercourse of gay and lesbian bodies articulates the redemptive meaning of the body's agency. If heterosexual marriage is understood in Christian tradition as an enactment of God's faithfulness and of the unity between Christ and the Church, and the means by which heterosexual bodies are taken into God's redemptive activity, how does this work for queer bodies in committed intimate relationships? McCarthy is not content to overlook sexuality and the sexual communication of the body in an overarching argument about mirroring God's faithfulness in relationship, important though that is, and as was apparent in the research findings. He is concerned that this emphasis circumvents the challenging question of difference between same-sex bodies that are moved by the desire for constancy of love. In what sense do same-sex couples receive their identity from, discover themselves in relation to, the embodied other?

For McCarthy, an understanding of sexual orientation is crucial to how we understand God's blessing in the sexual self-giving of same-sex couples one to another. He understands orientation to be a 'confluence of physical, psychological and social movements that bring an individual into being as a person' (2002, p.212). Just as men and women discover themselves through difference, so lesbians and gay men are 'persons who encounter the other (and so discover themselves) in relation to persons of the same sex. This same-sex orientation is a given of their coming to be...' (p.213). God's blessing and reconciliation come to us, same-sex couples and heterosexual couples, as we come into ourselves through God.

I end with this further exploration of the understanding of God's blessing experienced in same-sex relationships, since it is an example of the way in which queer theology opens doors into the layers of meaning in relationships such as those examined in this book, which fall outside the approved categories of heteronormative theology. Here, in this account of the redemptive quality of gay and lesbian sexual relationships, there is borrowed from the Christian tradition the rich conceptual understanding of the discovery of the self in God through sexual self-giving to the other. There is also a new queering of that tradition as gay and lesbian people 'come out' about their sexual desire for another in publicly communicative acts of loving commitment.

In conclusion

In this chapter, I have outlined arguments against same-sex marriage from a Christian perspective that are rooted in interpretations of Scripture and Church tradition. I suggest that the experience of lesbian and gay people may be used to challenge these sources and their interpretation, since moral truth, if it is to have authority, must resonate with the experience of its hearers in any given context, and with the whole tradition of Christian faith. I have demonstrated also that the gay and lesbian Christians involved in this study have wrestled in serious and knowledgeable ways with the meanings of

Scripture and Church tradition and have sought coherence with both in the living of their intimate and committed long-term relationships. They have concluded that, in the Christian desire for same-sex marriage, a new good is emerging to gradually challenge past logic about human sexuality. They concur with this quotation from Farley (2010), with which I end this chapter:

> When a deeply held conviction…grounded in our experience, appears to be contradicted by information from other sources, it must be tested against them. But if it continues to persuade us, continues to hold 'true', so that to deny it would do violence to our moral sensibilities, our affective capacity to respond to the good, and our very capacity for knowing, then it must function also as a measure against which the other sources are tested. (p.196)

Chapter 7

A SPACE FOR THE HEART

He can bring thy Summer out of Winter, though thou have no Spring.

John Donne

In the flat where I lived in 1990, I propped up a picture postcard of a desert in winter. Underneath the picture was the phrase cited above, 'He can bring thy Summer out of Winter, though thou have no Spring.' from a sermon by John Donne.[1] This was a scene in my kitchen thirty years ago, when I had recently met my partner, who with her lavender 2CV, black trilby, and brown leather rucksack brought spring. The loneliness of finding myself lesbian, yet detesting the ghettos and closets of the gay life then apparently on offer to me in a provincial city; the anxiety and depression involved in weathering the abhorrence of members of my family; the fear of facing the disapproval of conservative Christians; all these difficulties, which had for me created winter, paled into insignificance in the light of meeting someone worthy of my love who happened to love me. Those difficulties, save the first, raised their ugly heads from time to time, but nothing could hide the fact from myself, or from others, that I had been raised to an utterly new kind of life. Winter had become summer, almost overnight.

---

1   The sermon may be found at www.biblestudytools.com/classics/the-works-of-john-donne-vol-1/sermon-ii.html

For me as a Christian who seemingly by chance had happily collided with another Christian for a few hours at a weekend conference, this new partnership was experienced as an intervention by God for my healing, as a way to understand what the love of Christ feels like, as a raising to new life of faith and trust in another by the Holy Spirit. It has always been very difficult therefore to read or hear official statements of the Church of England proposing that what I found to be life-giving is the opposite. I had become used to this state of affairs, surviving or thriving by circling myself around with approving individuals and groups, even individual church congregations. Yet I had continued to live a split in my thinking between myself as 'good church person' and 'bad protesting lesbian'.

One significant result of pursuing this research, particularly the pursuit of the question of the theological meanings of same-sex marriage, which involves the detailed theological discussion of queer relationships, is the space and time it has afforded me to set my own experience of God-in-relationship in the context of queer theology. The work of Eugene Rogers, particularly, in his description of marriage, has helped me to articulate the sense I have always had that my relationship constitutes a significant act of God's creation: 'Marriage is in microcosm, a theatre of God's glory, a place where human beings – not just the spouses but also the neighbours – are allowed to witness creation as a significant act of God' (1999, p.214). I like the simple directness with which he writes that if there are gay and lesbian persons then God is committed to find means to bring them into an understanding of love, since that is what I sense happened to me. I had no such means of understanding love, and then they were provided. He helps me understand how difficult and indeed dangerous it may be to deny such a movement of God's Spirit, which it seems gay and lesbian Christians are frequently asked to do. What else is suppressed in our spiritual life, if the quickening of love, and its realization as a good, is suppressed, since 'The celebration, blessing and witnessing of a human wedding may catch up human beings by the Spirit into the very inner love and life of God' (Rogers 1999, p.196)?

In official statements of the Church of England, it has been suggested that lesbian and gay Christians question the goodness of experiences they have found to be for them the very sources of life and healing. Occasionally, such as in October 1998, when I had recently been inducted as the Rector of Soho, parish priests were asked to read these statements aloud to congregations after the main Sunday service of the week, as if they were the Word of God, a second sermon of the day. I was too embarrassed to do this, so conducted these readings quietly, inviting the congregation to join me, and to add their own interpretations and comments. This they did with healing laughter and guffaws about bishops and 'glass houses'. Kind jokes notwithstanding, the process was excruciatingly painful.

In interviews and reading for this project, I have been enabled to reflect on this painful experience, using it as a vantage point from which to reconfigure theology in two ways. In the first place, I have met Christians who have had the courage to defy the challenge to their entering civil partnership and marriage, but not to deny 'the reflex of a desiring God' (Rogers 1999, p.232). The pain of not being able to be both Church of England priest and legally married to my wife remains, but Jensen (2006) helpfully reminds me that I am married in all but the name of ecclesial law. I may therefore continue as a useful Althaus-Reid transformative 'alien', or 'voyeur' (2003, p.7) who has multiple passports within the system of the Church of England.

However, I also understand the meaning of this pain in a new way. In her queer demythologization of liberation theology, reflecting on the relationships between power, poverty and sexuality, Althaus-Reid complained that in the liberation theology of South America, heterosexuality had become 'sacralised to the point of not allowing it to be interrogated' (2003, p.130). In its many official statements, I see that the House of Bishops of the Church of England has become preoccupied with controlling sexuality. I understand, too, that when love is revealed in transgressive forms, as it is among my interviewees, heteronormative theology is threatened, because new faces of God become exposed. The myriad ways we understand God are revealed to be uncontrollable. My pain of being excluded continues to exist, but it is for me the route, which Althaus-Reid describes, to being 'surprised by God' (p.130).

Alison (2001) further transforms by his interpretation of the nature of this pain. For him, it is a sign that Christian belief and trust in God are not being used as power over another, to control them, or as the manipulative power of the victim, who claims the moral right of 'underdog'. He calls this position 'the space of the heart-close-to-cracking' (p.387). Here in this 'space of the heart' I recognize that I do not need to join in the game of agreement with the heteronormative theology of a controlling Church. Nor do I need to spend my life in angry, outraged protest. I may join in debate with those who will listen in that Church, not hoping to 'win', but to permit my 'emotional and mental structures [to] begin to absorb what is meant by the vivaciousness of the Creator God who brings into being and sustains all things' (p.391). I have a queer place to reside, in which that which is artificially sacred is to be continuously deconstructed, for a non-violent, loving, queer God to appear and act among us, God's people, to bless us in marriage.

References

Adams, M.M. (1996) 'Hurricane Spirits, Toppling Taboos.' In C. Hefling (ed.) *Our Selves, Our Souls and Bodies: Sexuality and the Household of God.* Boston, MA: Cowley Publications.

Alison, J. (1993) *Knowing Jesus.* London: SPCK.

Alison, J. (2001) *Faith Beyond Resentment: Fragments Catholic and Gay.* London: Darton, Longman and Todd.

Alison, J. (2002) 'Theology amidst the Stones and Dust.' In E.F. Rogers (ed.) *Theology and Sexuality: Classic and Contemporary Readings.* Oxford: Blackwell.

Alison, J. (2006) *Undergoing God: Dispatches from the Scene of a Break-In.* London: Darton, Longman and Todd.

Alison, J. (2007) 'The Gay Thing: Following the Still Small Voice', in G. Loughlin (ed.) *Queer Theology: Rethinking the Western Body.* Oxford: Blackwell.

Alison, J. (2010) *Broken Hearts and New Creations: Intimations of a Great Reversal.* London: Darton, Longman and Todd.

Althaus-Reid, M. (2000) *Indecent Theology.* London: Routledge.

Althaus-Reid, M. (2003) *The Queer God.* London: Routledge.

Althaus-Reid, M. (2004) *From Feminist Theology to Indecent Theology.* London: SCM Press.

Althaus-Reid, M. (2007) 'Demythologising Liberation Theology.' In C. Rowland (ed.) *Cambridge Companion to Liberation Theology* (2nd edn). Cambridge: Cambridge University Press.

Althaus-Reid, M. (2008) 'The Bi/Girl Writings: From Feminist Theology to Queer Theologies.' In L. Isherwood and K. McPhillips (eds) *Post-Christian Feminisms: A Critical Approach.* Aldershot: Ashgate.

Althaus-Reid, M. and Isherwood, L. (2004) 'Queering Theology.' In M. Althaus-Reid and L. Isherwood (eds) *The Sexual Theologian: Essays on Sex, God, and Politics*. London: T&T Clark International.

Althaus-Reid, M. and Isherwood, L. (2007) 'Thinking theology and queer theory.' *Feminist Theology 15*, 3, 302–314.

Bennett, Z. (2007) 'Action Is the Life of All: The Praxis-Eased Epistemology of Liberation Theology.' In C. Rowland (ed.) *Cambridge Companion to Liberation Theology* (2nd edn). Cambridge: Cambridge University Press.

Bennett, Z., Graham, E., Pattison, S. and Walton, H. (2018) *Invitation to Research in Practical Theology*. Abingdon: Routledge.

Braun, V. and Clarke, V. (2013) *Successful Qualitative Research*. London: Sage.

Butler, J. (1990) *Gender Trouble: Feminism and the Subversion of Identity*. London: Routledge.

Church of England (1991) *Issues in Human Sexuality: A Statement by the House of Bishops*. London: Church House Publishing.

Church of England (2005) *Civil Partnerships: A Pastoral Statement from the House of Bishops of the Church of England*. London: Church House Publishing.

Church of England (2012, 12 June) 'A Response to the Government Equalities Office Consultation "Equal Civil Marriage".' Anglican Communion News Service. Accessed on 11 November 2019 at www.anglicannews.org/news/2012/06/a-response-to-the-government-equalities-office-consultation-equal-civil-marriage.aspx

Church of England (2014) *House of Bishops Pastoral Guidance on Same-Sex Marriage*. London: Church House Publishing.

Coakley, S. (2013) *God, Sexuality and the Self*. Cambridge: Cambridge University Press.

Coakley, S. (2015) *The New Asceticism: Sexuality, Gender and the Quest for God*. London: Continuum.

Congregation for the Doctrine of the Faith (2003) *Considerations Regarding Proposals to Give Legal Recognition to Unions between Homosexual Persons*. Accessed on 11 November 2019 at www.vatican.va/roman_curia/congregations/cfaith/documents/rc_con_cfaith_doc_20030731_homosexual-unions_en.html

Cope, W. (2001) 'Being Boring.' In *If I Don't Know*. London: Faber and Faber.

Cornwall, S. (2011) *Controversies in Queer Theology*. London: SCM Press.

Davison, A. (2016) *Amazing Love: Theology for Understanding Discipleship, Sexuality and Mission*. London: DLT.

Diamond, L.M. (2008) *Sexual Fluidity: Understanding Women's Love and Desire*. Cambridge, MA: Harvard University Press.

Douglas, M. (1966) *Purity and Danger: An Analysis of Concepts of Purity and Taboo.* London: Routledge and Kegan Paul.

Fanthorpe, U.A. (1987) '7301.' In *A Watching Brief.* Calstock: Peterloo Poets.

Farley, M.A. (2010) *Just Love: A Framework for Christian Sexual Ethics.* London: Continuum.

Ford, D. (1999) *Self and Salvation: Being Transformed.* Cambridge: Cambridge University Press.

Ford, M. (2019) *God, Gender, Sex and Marriage.* London: Jessica Kingsley Publishers.

Gearhart, S. and Johnson, W.R. (eds) (1974) *Loving Women/Loving Men: Gay Liberation and the Church.* San Francisco, CA: Glide.

Giddens, A. (1991) *Modernity and Self-Identity: Self and Society in the Late Modern Age.* Cambridge: Polity Press.

Giddens, A. (1992) *The Transformation of Intimacy: Sexuality, Love and Eroticism in Modern Stories.* Cambridge: Polity Press.

Girard, R. (2001) *I Saw Satan Fall Like Lightning.* Leominster: Gracewing.

Goss, R.E. (1993) *Jesus Acted Up: A Gay and Lesbian Manifesto.* San Francisco, CA: Harper.

Government Equalities Office (2012) *Equal Civil Marriage: A Consultation.* London: HMSO.

Guttiérez, G. (1971) *Teología de la liberación,* translated 1973 as *A Theology of Liberation.* New York: Orbis Books.

Hanks, T. (1997) 'A Family Friend: Paul's Letter to the Romans as a Source of Affirmation for Queers and their Families.' In R.E Goss and A. Adams Squire Strongheart (eds) *Our Families, Our Values: Snapshots of Queer Kinship,* Binghampton, NY: The Haworth Press.

Hefling, C. (ed.) (1996) *Our Selves, Our Souls and Bodies.* Boston, MA: Cowley Publications.

Hensher, P. (2014) *The Emperor Waltz.* London: Fourth Estate.

Hensman, S. (2015) *Sexuality, Struggle and Saintliness.* London: Ekklesia.

Hunt, M. (1991) *Fierce Tenderness: A Feminist Theology of Friendship.* New York, NY: Crossroad.

Hutton, A. (2015, 15 December) 'Civil partnerships: Ten years on.' BBC News online. Accessed on 11 November 2019 at www.bbc.co.uk/news/uk-35136125

Jensen, D.H. (2006) 'God's desire for us: Reformed theology and the question of same-sex marriage.' *Theology 109,* 847, 12–20.

John, J. (2012) *Permanent, Faithful, Stable: Christian Same-Sex Marriage.* London: Darton, Longman and Todd.

Kinsey, A.C., Pomeroy, W. and Martin, C. (1948) *Sexual Behavior in the Human Male.* Philadelphia, PA: W.B. Saunders.

Koch, T.R. (2006) 'Isaiah.' In D. Guest, R.E. Goss, M. West and T. Bohache (eds) *The Queer Bible Commentary*. London: SCM Press.

Kolakowski, V.S. (1997) 'The Concubine and the Eunuch: Queering Up the Breeder's Bible.' In R.E Goss and A. Adams Squire Strongheart (eds) *Our Families, Our Values: Snapshots of Queer Kinship*, Binghampton, NY: The Haworth Press.

Livingstone, M. (2010) *Kitaj* (4th edn). London and New York: Phaidon Press.

Loughlin, G. (ed.) (2007) *Queer Theology: Rethinking the Western Body*. Oxford: Blackwell.

Lowry, R. (ed.) (1869) 'How Can I Keep from Singing?' Hymn no. 16. In *Bright Jewels for the Sunday School*. New York, NY: Biglow and Main.

Macourt, M. (1977) *Towards a Theology of Gay Liberation*. London: SCM Press.

Maraschin, J. (2009) 'Worship and the Excluded.' In M. Althaus-Reid (ed.) *Liberation Theology and Sexuality* (2nd edn). London: SCM Press.

May, T. (2001) *Social Research: Issues, Methods and Process* (3rd edn). Maidenhead: Open University Press.

McCarthy, D.M. (2002) 'The Relationship of Bodies: A Nuptial Hermeneutics of Same-Sex Unions.' In E.F. Rogers (ed.) *Theology and Sexuality: Classic and Contemporary Readings*. Oxford: Blackwell.

McCarthy, D.M. (2007) 'Fecundity: Sex and Social Reproduction.' In G. Loughlin (ed.) *Queer Theology: Rethinking the Western Body*. Oxford: Blackwell.

McFague, S. (1975) *Speaking in Parables*. Philadelphia, PA: Fortress Press.

McNeill, J.J. (1976) *The Church and the Homosexual*. Boston, MA: Beacon Press.

Merton, T. (1985) Untitled Poem in *Eighteen Poems*. New York, NY: New Directions.

Miller-McLemore, B.J. (1993) 'The human web: Reflections on the state of pastoral theology.' *Christian Century 110*, 366–369.

O'Donovan, O. (2009) *A Conversation Waiting to Begin: The Churches and the Gay Controversy*. London: SCM Press.

Ozanne, J. (ed.) (2016) *Journeys in Grace and Truth: Revisiting Scripture and Sexuality*. London: Via Media.

Pastoral Constitution on the Church and the Modern World (1965) *Gaudium et Spes*. Vatican Council Documents.

Perry, T. (1972) *The Lord Is My Shepherd and He Knows I'm Gay: The Autobiography of the Reverend Troy Perry*. Los Angeles, CA: Nash Publishing.

Ratzinger, J. (1969) 'The Transmission of Divine Revelation.' In H. Vorgrimler (ed.) *Commentary on the Documents of Vatican II, vol. 3*. New York, NY: Herder and Herder.

Rogers, E.F. (1999) *Sexuality and the Christian Body: The Way into the Triune God*. Oxford: Blackwell.

Rogers, E.F. (ed.) (2002) *Theology and Sexuality: Classic and Contemporary Readings*. Oxford: Blackwell.

Rogers, E.F. (2009) 'Paul on Exceeding Nature: Queer Gentiles and the Giddy Gardener.' In F.S. Roden (ed.) *Jewish, Christian, Queer: Crossroads and Identities*. Aldershot: Ashgate.

Rowland, C. (ed.) (2007) *Cambridge Companion to Liberation Theology* (2nd edn). Cambridge: Cambridge University Press.

Rudy, K. (1997) *Sex and the Church: Homosexuality and the Transformation of Christian Ethics*. Boston, MA: Beacon Press.

Ruether, R.R. (1993) *Sexism and God-talk: Toward a Feminist Theology*. Boston, MA: Beacon Press.

Song, R. (2014) *Covenant Calling: Towards a Theology of Same-Sex Relationships*. London: SCM Press.

Stone, K. (2004) 'Queering the Canaanite.' In M. Althaus-Reid and L. Isherwood (eds) *The Sexual Theologian: Essays on God, Sex and Politics*. London: T&T Clark.

Stuart, E. (2003) *Gay and Lesbian Theologies: Repetitions with Critical Difference*. Aldershot: Ashgate.

Stuart, E. (2007) 'Sacramental Flesh.' In G. Loughlin (ed.) *Queer Theology: Rethinking the Western Body*. Oxford: Blackwell.

Thatcher, A. (2011) *God, Sex and Gender: An Introduction*. London: Wiley-Blackwell.

Vasey, M. (1995) *Strangers and Friends: A New Exploration of Homosexuality and the Bible*. London: Hodder and Stoughton.

Vatican Report of the Synod on the Family (2014) English text available at www.catholicherald.co.uk/news/2014/10/30/full-text-official-translation-of-final-synod-report

Volf, M. (2010) *Captive to the Word of God*. Cambridge: Eerdmans.

Ward, G. (1999) 'Bodies: The Displaced Body of Jesus Christ.' In J. Milbank, C. Pickstock and G. Ward (eds) *Radical Orthodoxy: A New Theology*. London: Routledge.

Wells, S. (2015) *A Nazareth Manifesto*. Oxford: Wiley-Blackwell.

Wells, S. (2016) *How Then Shall We Live?* Norwich: Canterbury Press.

Williams, R. (1994) *Open to Judgement: Sermons and Addresses*. London: Darton, Longman and Todd.

Williams, R. (1996) 'The Body's Grace.' In C. Hefling (ed.) *Our Selves, Our Souls and Bodies: Sexuality and the Household of God*. Boston, MA: Cowley Publications.

Williams, R. (2003) 'Knowing Myself in Christ.' In T. Bradshaw (ed.) *The Way Forward? Christian Voices on Homosexuality and the Church* (2nd edn). London: SCM Press.

Wilson, A. (2014) *More Perfect Union: Understanding Same-Sex Marriage.* London: Darton, Longman and Todd.

Wilson, N. (1995) *Our Tribe: Queer Folks, God, Jesus and the Bible.* San Francisco, CA: Harper.